The Secret of Room 401

ADULT LEARNER SERIES

The Secret of Room 401

JUDITH ANDREWS GREEN
DIRECTOR,
ADULT BASIC EDUCATION
MAINE SCHOOL DISTRICT #17

 JAMESTOWN PUBLISHERS

Catalog No. 204

The Secret of Room 401

Cover Design by Stephen R. Anthony
Cover Illustration and
Story Illustrations by Janet Watt

Printed in the United States of America

6 7 8 9   99 98 97 96

ISBN 0-89061-210-2

Titles in This Series

No. 200, Murder by Radio
No. 201, The Man Who Stopped Time
No. 202, The Man with the Scar
No. 203, Dr. Valdez
No. 204, The Secret of Room 401
No. 205, A City for Ransom
No. 206, Nightmare Snow
No. 207, Peril on the Road
No. 208, Killer in a Trance?

For my mother
with love

To the Reader

Rick Tardif had been in a car crash. Now he lay in a hospital bed. He might never walk again. He had nothing to live for.

Then he saw someone come into his room and give a signal.

Rick had to find out what was happening. This is the story of how he found out the secret of room 401 — and what happened when he did.

Before each chapter of the story, there are words for you to look at and learn. These words are in sentences so you can see how they will be used in the story. After each chapter there are questions for you to answer. These questions will give you an idea of how well you are reading.

Next come lessons that will help you to read, write and spell better. Other lessons tell you things you need to know about, and know how to do, to get along in life.

The answers to all the questions and exercises are in the back of the book. This lets you check your answers to see if they are right.

We hope you will like reading *The Secret of Room 401* and learning all of the things this book teaches.

Contents

How to Use This Book

1. Learn the Preview Words

Say the words in the box. Then read the sentences. Try to learn the words. See if you know what each sentence means.

2. Read the Chapter

As you read, try to follow the story and what the people in it are doing. See how Rick solves the secret of Room 401.

3. Answer: Comprehension Questions

Put an *x* in the box next to the best answer to each question. Read all ten questions first and answer the easy ones. Then go back and answer the hard ones.

4. Correct Your Answers

Use the Answer Key on page 203. If your answer is wrong, circle that box and put an x in the right box.

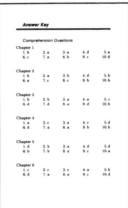

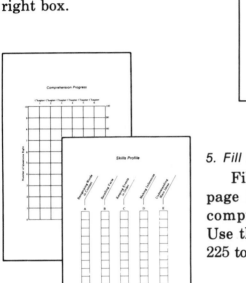

5. Fill in the Graphs

Fill in the graph on page 223 to show your comprehension score. Use the graph on page 225 to chart your skills.

6. Read: Language Skills

This comes after the questions. Read the pages and do the exercises. Use the Answer Key on page 204 to correct the exercises.

7. Read: Understanding Life Skills

Read these pages and follow the step-by-step lessons. Use the Answer Key on page 213 to check your answers.

8. Practice: Applying Life Skills

Read the instructions and do the Life Skills exercise. Take your time. Do the work carefully. Try to remember what you just read about understanding life skills. Use the Answer Key on page 217 to correct the exercise.

9. Read the Chapter Again

Go back to the story and read it once more. This time, as you read, try to feel all the interest and excitement the writer has built in.

Then, go on to the Preview Words for the next chapter.

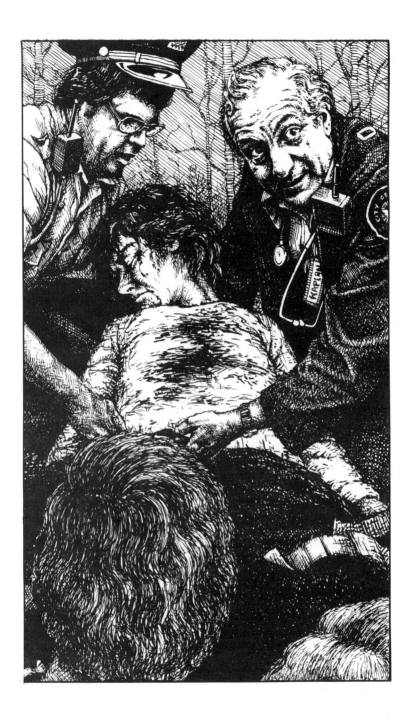

1

Into the Darkness

Study the words in the box. Then read the sentences below with your teacher. Look carefully at the words with lines under them.

accident	emergency	metal	stretcher
ambulance	enough	radio	torch
bleeding	guy	silver	wheelchair
curve	headlights	siren	wrecker
elevator	hospital	strange	X-ray

1. The <u>headlights</u> of the car made the road shine.
2. They shone on the <u>silver</u> lines of rain.
3. The <u>curve</u> in the road would be coming up soon.
4. What's keeping that <u>ambulance</u>?
5. He made the call on the <u>radio</u>.
6. He isn't <u>bleeding</u> too badly.
7. "I'll call a <u>wrecker</u>," the policeman said.
8. Just then they could hear a <u>siren</u>.
9. Oh, no! The poor <u>guy</u>!
10. Bring a <u>torch</u>—we're going to have to cut him out.
11. They cut away the crushed <u>metal</u>.
12. At last the hole was big <u>enough</u>.
13. They called for a <u>stretcher</u>.
14. We'll radio ahead to the <u>hospital</u>.
15. The people in the <u>emergency</u> room were waiting.
16. They rolled him right to the <u>X-ray</u> room.
17. You were in a car <u>accident</u>.
18. They put him in a <u>strange</u>-looking bed.
19. A <u>wheelchair</u> was standing next to her.
20. She sped over to the <u>elevator</u>.

It didn't seem like a night that would change your life.

Rick Tardif had got off work late again. He had run out to his car. It was raining hard, and he was in a hurry. But, he thought, it was a night like any other night.

He didn't know that nothing would ever be the same again.

He pulled out of the parking lot fast. He had a date with Kelly that night. He had to get washed up. He had to grab some supper, too. So much to do! He was going to be late. Kelly would be mad at him.

The headlights of the car made the wet road shine. They shone on the silver lines of rain. They made a soft glow of light in the fog. The headlights in the rain were kind of nice. If you thought about it, the night was almost pretty.

But Rick wasn't thinking about it. He stepped on the gas. The car rushed on into the dark.

The headlights cut through the darkness. They shone on the rain in silver lines. It really was kind of pretty. If Rick had known what was going to happen to him, he might have thought about it. But all he thought about was his date.

He stepped down harder on the gas. The car sped down the wet road. The rain was coming down even harder.

The big curve in the road would be coming up soon . . . . Sooner than he thought.

Rick knew that curve well. He knew there was a steep bank beside it. He knew that he should slow down.

But tonight he wasn't thinking about the curve. He was thinking about his supper. What should he eat? What would be quick? In his mind, he was at home, eating supper. Not out on the road, going into that curve.

The headlights were shining on the wet road. Suddenly they were shining on trees! Rick came to. The curve! In a second he would be off the road! He would go down over the bank! He threw the steering wheel over. The headlights swung around. They shone on the road again—just for a second. Then they shone on the trees again as the car spun around.

Rick threw the wheel over the other way. The car rocked and turned. The headlights shone on the road—the trees—the road—the trees. The tires grabbed, then slid.

For a second, the headlights shone on nothing but air. The car slid over the side of the bank. Down, down. Crash! The car hit the bank and rolled. The headlights went out. The car rolled again, then came to a stop on its roof.

Everything was dark. And quiet.

*   *   *   *   *

A little later, a police car was driving by. "Look!" the driver said. "Look at those tire marks! They weren't there before, were they?"

"No, they weren't!" the other policeman said. "Look—someone has gone right over the edge!"

Quickly, the policemen pulled over. They jumped out and ran through the rain to look. They hoped that they would see nothing.

But there it was. Down at the bottom of the drop-off. In the glow of light from the police car, they could see something. Yes, it was a car—what was left of it.

"I'll call for an ambulance!" one policeman said. He ran back to the police car to use the radio.

The other policeman was already climbing down over the bank. He headed for the car.

It was crushed in on every side. The roof was crushed down. "I don't think anyone could be alive in there," the policeman said to himself. He got down in the mud and looked in the car window.

"Can you see anyone? Are they alive?" the other policeman called as he climbed down to the wrecked car.

"The driver is a man. I don't see anyone else."

"How does he look?"

"I don't know. He isn't bleeding too badly. But I can't tell if he's breathing," the first policeman said. "Let's see if we can get this door open." They pulled on the door. It wouldn't move.

"I'll call a wrecker," the second policeman said. "We're going to have to get them to cut him out of there." He climbed back up the muddy bank and ran to the police car again.

He made the call. Then he called down, "I'll wait up here for the ambulance. How is he doing?"

"I don't know," the other policeman called. "I still can't tell if he's alive or not. I hope that ambulance gets here soon."

Minute after long minute went by. Then they could hear a siren. Red lights flashed in the dark. The ambulance pulled up and stopped. Two men jumped out. One ran to the back of the ambulance and started to pull out bags. The other ran up to the policeman who was waiting. "Where is it?" he asked.

"Down there. One man. We can't tell if he's breathing or not. We're going to have to get someone to cut him out."

"Did you call a wrecker?" the ambulance driver asked.

"He's on the way."

"Good." The man climbed down the bank. He tried to get the door open. Then he tried the other doors. At last he got one open. He climbed into the car. Carefully, he touched Rick's face. "He's alive!" he called. "He's breathing OK! Get that wrecker down here!"

The wrecker pulled up. Another man climbed quickly down the bank. He looked at the crushed door. "This is going to be a real job," he said. He bent down to talk to the ambulance man in the car. "What do you think? Can you get him out that way?"

"I don't dare to. Look at the way he's lying. He may have broken his back."

"Oh, no! The poor guy! Well, let's get going." He called up to the men by the truck. "Bring a torch down here. We're going to have to cut him out. We're going to have to make a lot of room. It looks like we've got a broken back down here."

Slowly, carefully, they turned the torch on the car. Bit by bit, they cut away the crushed metal. When the hole was big enough, they called for a stretcher.

The men from the ambulance climbed into the car with the stretcher. They put the stretcher right next to Rick. Slowly, slowly, they picked him up, being careful not to move his back. They put him down on the stretcher just the way he had been lying. They strapped him down. Then one of them climbed out of the car again.

"OK, let's have some help here," he said. The policemen helped to pull the stretcher out of the car. They took it up the bank to the ambulance.

They put the stretcher into the ambulance. One of the men climbed in with it. The other closed the doors. Then he turned to the policemen. "We'll radio ahead to the hospital. See you." He ran to get in the front of the ambulance.

"What do you think?" a policeman called after him. "Is he going to make it?"

"He may make it," the ambulance driver said. "But if he does live, he won't walk again." The ambulance pulled out. It was gone in a flash of red lights.

"There are some days I hate this job," the policeman said.

*   *   *   *   *

The ambulance pulled up at the hospital. The people in the emergency room were waiting for it.

They put Rick's stretcher on wheels. They rolled him right to the X-ray room. They took the X-ray pictures without moving him. Then they rolled the stretcher out to wait for the pictures to be ready.

Rick began to wake up. Where was he? What had happened? There were so many lights . . . . There were so many people rushing around . . . . What was going on?

A nurse was standing by Rick. She saw him move his head. She bent over him. "Are you awake?" she asked.

"Yes . . . I think so," Rick said slowly. It was hard to talk. "Where am I? What happened?"

"You're in the hospital," the nurse said. "You were

in a car accident. Try not to move. How do you feel?"

"I . . . I can't feel my legs. Hey! I can't feel my legs!" Rick said. "Are they still there?" He tried to sit up, but the straps held him down.

The nurse held his head down. "Try not to move," she said again. "Yes, your legs are still there. They're all right. Everything will be all right."

"Why can't I feel them? Why? What has happened to me?"

"We're waiting for the X-rays now," the nurse said. "Just rest. Everything will be all right."

Rick lay quietly. He felt as if the world were coming to an end. What could he do? What would happen to him?

Then the doctors came in. One had the big X-ray pictures in his hand. "Is he awake?" he asked. "That's good." He held up one of the pictures. "His head seems to be all right. How do you feel?" he asked Rick.

"My legs! I can't feel them!" Rick said.

"Yes, . . ." the doctor said sadly. "I'm sorry to have to tell you this." He held up some more pictures. "Your back is broken."

"What does that mean? Can you fix it?" Rick asked.

"No, we can't fix it," the doctor said. "It will heal some. We don't know how much. Time will tell."

"You mean . . . I might not walk again?" Rick asked.

"I'm afraid not," the doctor said. "But only time will tell."

The doctors checked Rick over carefully. They took care of his cuts. Then a nurse washed him. Then she rolled his stretcher down a long hall.

All this time, Rick didn't say anything. He didn't even watch what the doctors were doing. He didn't see where the nurse was taking him. He just kept thinking about what the doctor had said. The words kept going around in his head. "I might not walk again. I might not walk again. Only time will tell. Only time will tell."

At last the stretcher stopped. Suddenly Rick saw faces hanging over him. It was his mother and father.

His mother was crying. His father looked as if he had been crying, too. But now he was trying to smile.

"Oh, Rick!" his mother cried. "Rick! Are you all right? Does it hurt? Oh, my baby!"

His father put his arm around her. "Now, May," he said. "Of course he's all right. Everything will be all right." He reached out and touched Rick softly on the hand. "Everything will be all right," he said again.

"No, it won't, Dad!" Rick said. "I can't feel my legs! They said I might not walk again!"

"Of course you will. Of course you will. Everything will be all right. It just takes time, that's all."

The words went around in Rick's head again. Only time will tell.

"I'll have to put him in his bed now," the nurse said.

Rick's father said, "OK. We'll go. We just wanted to see him." He touched Rick's hand again. "Good night, Rick. We'll see you in the morning. Don't worry. Everything will be all right." He turned to go.

"Hey, Dad," Rick said. "Will you call Kelly for me? I had a date with her tonight. Tell her — Tell her I

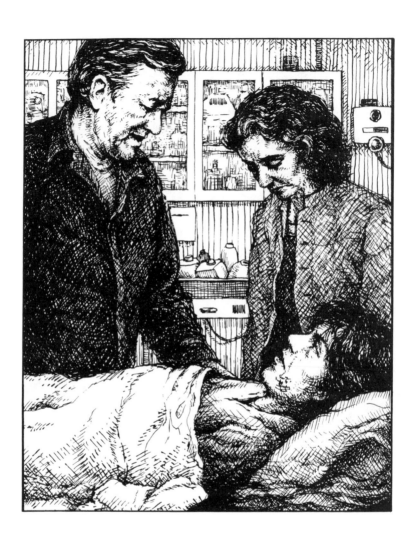

won't make it."

"Sure, Son. I'll tell her," Rick's father said. "Come on, May. Let's go. The guy needs his rest."

"Good night, dear," his mother said. She bent down and kissed him softly. "Try to get some sleep."

Their faces were gone. Rick could hear them walking away down the hall. Then the stretcher was rolling again.

"Put him in Room 401," a nurse said. A few minutes later, the stretcher turned and went through a door. He was in a room. More nurses came in. Slowly, carefully, they put him on a strange-looking bed. Something was put around him. Something else was put around his head. He couldn't move.

A nurse gave him a pill. "This will help you sleep," she said.

Sleep came quickly. But one last time, he could hear in his head the doctor saying it. "Only time will tell...."

*   *   *   *   *

At the other end of the hall, a woman was lying in her bed. A wheelchair was standing next to her.

The woman was talking on the phone. "How are you today, dear?" she was asking.

"I'm fine, Grandmother," said the little girl at the other end of the line. "I made something for you today."

"How nice. When will I get to see it?"

"Dad says we can come to see you tomorrow."

"Oh, good. I'll be waiting for you. Sleep well, dear."

"Good night, Grandmother."

The woman put down the phone. Then she reached under her pillow. She pulled out a pipe. She lit the pipe and lay back, smiling. Soon there was smoke all around her.

A nurse came in. "Oh, Alice!" the nurse said. "One of these days you're going to burn this hospital right down!"

Alice just smiled. She gave the pipe to the nurse. "Will you help me into my wheelchair, my dear?" she asked. "I'd like to take a little spin."

"All right," the nurse said. "But don't go too far. You need your rest, you know." She lifted the woman into her wheelchair. Then she pushed her out into the hall. "Now, be careful," she said.

"I will," Alice said. She rolled her wheelchair slowly down the hall. But as soon as the nurse was out of sight, she turned around. She sped over to the elevator. The doors opened, and she rolled her wheelchair in.

A few minutes later, she was in the basement. With a big smile on her face, she headed for the coffee shop.

*   *   *   *   *

In another part of the hospital, someone else was on the phone. "Hello? Steve? This is Ed."

"What's up?" asked the man at the other end of the line.

"I don't know what to do. They put someone in Room 401."

"They did? Well, we'll have to change things around. Can you use another room?"

"I don't know," said the man named Ed. "401 is the only one you can see really well from the outside."

"Well, what about this guy in the room? How bad off is he?" Steve asked.

"Broken back, I think. They'll give him a pill tonight."

"Then we're OK for tonight. We can go ahead with it tonight. After that, we'll just have to play it by ear. The guy may be pretty well out of it for a while."

"What if he's wide awake?" Ed asked.

"Then we'll just have to wait till they move him," Steve said. "Of course, you could always put him to sleep...."

"Hey! You said that no one would get hurt! That guy has a broken back! He doesn't need to get hit again!" Ed said.

"OK, OK," Steve said. "Don't worry about it. Just do your thing tonight. Then keep in touch."

"I will. See you later."

"Right."

*   *   *   *   *

Rick slept all through the night.

He didn't hear Alice go by on her way to the elevator.

And, later, he didn't hear someone come into his

room. He didn't feel someone standing over him. He didn't see someone go to the window. He didn't see someone put the window shade up. And pull it down again. Three times.

Directions. Answer these questions about the chapter you have just read. Put an *x* in the box beside the best answer to each question.

1. (E) Rick didn't slow down when he went around the curve because

   ☐ a. he didn't know the road very well.
   ☐ b. he wasn't thinking about what he was doing.
   ☐ c. he was going to call the ambulance.
   ☐ d. he didn't like to drive slowly.

2. (C) What happened right after the policemen looked at the wrecked car?

   ☐ a. They called an ambulance.
   ☐ b. They called a wrecker.
   ☐ c. The ambulance pulled up.
   ☐ d. They put Rick on a stretcher.

3. (D) The policeman said, "There are some days I hate this job." This was because

   ☐ a. he felt so bad that Rick was hurt.
   ☐ b. he got all muddy climbing down to Rick's car.
   ☐ c. he wished that he could drive an ambulance.
   ☐ d. he didn't like to work at night.

4. (E) In the hospital, Rick felt afraid because

☐ a. the doctors took X-rays of him.
☐ b. he was bleeding badly from his cuts.
☐ c. he didn't like hospitals.
☐ d. he couldn't feel his legs.

5. (A) The doctor told Rick, *"Only time will tell."* What does this mean?

☐ a. He would have to wait to find out.
☐ b. He would have to look at a clock.
☐ c. He found out his clock had stopped.
☐ d. He would never find out what happened.

6. (C) When Rick saw his mother and father, what happened last?

☐ a. His mother kissed him.
☐ b. His mother started to cry.
☐ c. Rick asked them to call Kelly.
☐ d. He told them he might not walk again.

7. (D) Rick was put into a strange-looking bed that kept him from moving. This was done because

☐ a. his back had to be kept straight so that it would heal.
☐ b. the police wanted to make sure that he couldn't get away.
☐ c. the doctors were afraid that he would get up and walk.
☐ d. the X-rays showed that he had hurt his head in the accident.

8. (B) Alice got the nurse upset by

☐ a. calling her names.
☐ b. smoking a pipe.
☐ c. going to see Rick.
☐ d. talking on the phone.

9. (A) Alice said, "Will you help me into my wheelchair? I'd like to *take a little spin.*" What did she mean?

☐ a. She wanted to turn around and around in her wheelchair.
☐ b. She wanted to take the little wheels off her wheelchair.
☐ c. She wanted to go for a short ride in her wheelchair.
☐ d. She wanted to go for a short ride in Rick's car.

10. (B) The man on the telephone knew that Rick would sleep that night because

☐ a. he was very tired from the accident.
☐ b. he was very tired from working late.
☐ c. it was very quiet in the hospital.
☐ d. he would get a pill to make him sleep.

Skills Used to Answer Questions

A. Recognizing Words in Context   B. Recalling Facts
C. Keeping Events in Order   D. Making Inferences
            E. Understanding Main Ideas

Capital Letters for People's Names

Use a capital letter for the first letter of a person's name. Here are three examples:

<u>M</u>aria   <u>J</u>oe   <u>K</u>im

Use a capital letter for a person's last name too. Here are three examples:

<u>M</u>aria <u>G</u>arcia   <u>J</u>oe <u>J</u>ones   <u>K</u>im <u>W</u>ong

And use a capital letter for a person's middle name. Here are three examples. Each person has three names. Each name begins with a capital letter.

<u>M</u>aria <u>C</u>oncepcion <u>G</u>arcia

<u>J</u>oe <u>W</u>illie <u>J</u>ones

<u>K</u>im <u>L</u>ee <u>W</u>ong

Some people have last names with two parts. Each part begins with a capital letter. Here are two examples:

<u>R</u>ip <u>V</u>an <u>W</u>inkle   <u>L</u>eonardo <u>D</u>a <u>V</u>inci

Sometimes people do not use their whole names. They use only the first letters of their names. The first letter is an *initial.* An initial is always a capital letter. It is always followed by a period.

In the name Susan <u>B</u>. Anthony, <u>B</u>. is the initial. Find the initial in the name below. Write the initial and the period on the line next to the name.

Harry S. Truman _____

You often have to print your name on papers and applications. Sometimes you have to give your whole name, including your middle name. Sometimes you just have to print the initial of your middle name.

The form below shows Maria Garcia's name printed correctly. On this form she gave her whole name. She followed the directions under the name line.

Garcia Maria Concepcion
NAME: last   first   middle

On the second form, Maria had to use only her middle initial. See how she followed the directions on the line below the name line.

Garcia Maria C.
NAME: last   first   middle initial

Now fill in Kim Lee Wong's name on the two forms below. Follow the directions under the name lines. They tell you where to print each part of the name. And they tell you whether to use a middle name or just a middle initial.

NAME: last   first   middle

NAME: last   first   middle initial

Exercise 1

This exercise gives the names of Presidents of the United States. Find each name and each initial. Then print it in the space below the sentence. Begin each name with a capital letter. Use a capital letter for each initial, and use a period after it. The first name has been filled in for you.

1. The first president was george washington.

   <u>*George*</u>   <u>*Washington*</u>

2. The second president was john adams.

   _____   _____

3. The third president was thomas jefferson.

   _____   _____

4. The sixth president was john quincy adams.

   _____ _____ _____

5. The eighth president was martin van buren.

   _____ _____ _____

6. The president during the Civil War was abraham lincoln.

   _____   _____

7. The president during World War I was woodrow wilson.

   _____   _____

8. President warren g. harding died in office.

_____ _____ _____

9. Two presidents were cousins: theodore roosevelt

_____ _____

and franklin d. roosevelt.

_____ _____ _____

10. Sometimes franklin d. roosevelt was known by his initials. Print his initials below. Be sure to use the periods.

_____ _____ _____

Exercise 2

This exercise uses the names of people who are not so famous. Find each name and each initial. Print them on the lines below each sentence. Begin each name with a capital letter.

Use a capital letter and a period for each initial. Only two names have initials.

The first name has been printed for you.

1. My sister saw james r. grundy.

_____ _James R. Grundy_ _____

2. The car belongs to abe klein.

_____

3. Give the book to dorothy goodrich.

_____

4. Who was marie curie?

_____

5. Give the keys to david del pozzo.

_____

6. Did you call richard almy last week?

_____

7. I met diane healy yesterday.

_____

8. She heard paul gallagher sing.

_____

9. Is bernadette de rosa coming?

_____

10. elizabeth t. ethier sent the money.

_____

Reading the Food Section of the Newspaper

The food section is a part of your newspaper that gives you information about food. Usually the food section is in the Wednesday paper. The food section has articles that tell you many things about food. Some articles tell you about foods that are good for you. Other articles tell you about how to cook food and how to save money when you buy food.

The Wednesday food section also has advertisements, or ads, from nearby supermarkets. The ads tell you what foods are on sale now. The ads can help you save money on food.

The *index* of the newspaper tells you how to find the food section. The index is a list of the articles that are in the paper. This list also tells you what pages the articles are found on. The sample newspaper index below tells you where the food section is.

Index

The food section is in Section C. This is the third section of the paper. The index also tells you on what page of Section C the food articles begin.

Now you can find the food section. It has its own index or list of articles and pages. The sample food section index shows you how an index helps you.

Food

Look at the food index. It gives you the titles of food articles and the pages on which you can find the articles. Fill in each blank. Print the page number for each article on the line after each title.

1. Eat To Get Better: *Page*————————

2. Cooking for One or Two: *Page* ——————

3. Budget Meals: *Page*————————

4. Children's Cooking: *Page* _____

Look at the food index again. Fill in each blank. Print the title of each article on the line after each page number. The first one has been done for you.

5. Page C-3: *Smart Shopping*

6. Page C-5: _____

7. Page C-1: _____

8. Page C-6: _____

Using the Food Section of the Newspaper

You can learn more about food by reading the Wednesday food section of your newspaper. The *index* of the food section helps you find articles. It is a list of articles and the pages on which you find them. The list below is the food section index you have used before.

Food

Pretend you have some questions about food. Pretend you want to read just one article to find an answer to each question.

Read each question. Then look at the index. Choose

one article to help you answer each question. Print the page number of each article on the line after each question. The first one has been done for you.

1. What should I cook for the party?

   Page ___C-7___

2. How can I make good choices of fresh vegetables?

   Page _____

3. What will be good to have when I am eating alone?

   Page _____

4. What is simple enough for a child to learn to cook?

   Page _____

5. How can I plan meals that don't cost too much?

   Page _____

6. What wine should I serve with chicken?

   Page _____

7. What foods will help me get better after my heart attack?

   Page _____

8. What lunches will help me lose weight?

   Page _____

2

Out the Window

Study the words in the box. Then read the sentences below with your teacher. Look carefully at the words with lines under them.

backbone	friends	lower	spinal
body	half	mirror	thoughts
bottles	heard	questions	tubes
buckled	helpless	relax	wondered
Dr.	hour	remembered	worse

1. Something kept pulling at his <u>thoughts</u>.
2. Then he <u>remembered</u> it all.
3. There was a <u>mirror</u> in front of his face.
4. She <u>buckled</u> straps all around him.
5. I'm going to turn you over. Try to <u>relax</u>.
6. There were <u>bottles</u> hung up around him.
7. There were <u>tubes</u> going into him from the bottles.
8. He couldn't move. He was <u>helpless</u>.
9. "Hello," he said. "I'm <u>Dr.</u> Rains."
10. You must have a lot of <u>questions</u>.
11. Your spinal cord is in your <u>backbone</u>.
12. The <u>spinal</u> cord connects the body to the brain.
13. Your brain is not in touch with the <u>lower</u> half of you.
14. So you can't feel the lower <u>half</u> of you.
15. We can keep it from getting <u>worse</u>.
16. Your <u>body</u> isn't meant to lie still.
17. Every <u>hour</u>, the nurse turned him over.
18. Suddenly Rick <u>heard</u> a sound.
19. No! I don't want my <u>friends</u> to come!
20. "Oh, I just <u>wondered</u>," Rick said.

Rick began to wake up. He still felt very sleepy. He didn't open his eyes. He lay still and tried to wake up.

He felt very strange. He was lying face down, with his arms hanging down. Why was he lying this way? He wasn't in his bed. Where was he? He tried to think. But he was so sleepy.... He almost went back to sleep.

Something kept pulling at his thoughts. What was it? He just couldn't think.

Suddenly, he knew what it was. It was two things. He could not move. And he could not feel his legs.

He woke up fast. His eyes opened wide.

He still couldn't move. There was something around his head. His body was held down tightly. And his legs! Where were they?

He started to shout, to call for help. Then he remembered.

It all came back to him at once. He remembered it all. Driving home from work in the rain. Being in a hurry. Going into the curve. Going off the road. And then waking up in the hospital.

He remembered something else, too. He remembered what the doctor had said.

He might never walk again.

He was afraid. He was more afraid than he had ever been before. Would it be like this from now on? Would he spend the rest of his life here? Would he spend the rest of his life lying on a hospital bed? He felt more and more afraid.

Just then someone came into the room. He moved

his eyes up. There was a mirror in front of his face. In the mirror he could see a nurse.

"Hello, Mr. Tardif," she said. "How are you feeling?"

Rick couldn't talk at first. It took him a minute to beat down the fear which had filled him. At last he said, "Hello."

The nurse smiled at him. Then she began to work around him. He couldn't see her in the mirror any more. He tried to turn his head to see what she was doing.

"Try not to move," the nurse said. "It will take you a while to get used to all this. But you must try to hold still." She came up to his head again. "I'm going to turn you over now. Try to relax. You'll be all right."

The nurse put a pad over his back. Then she put a big metal frame over that. She strapped it to the bed he was lying on. She buckled straps all around him.

"I'm going to turn you now. Just relax. Don't worry. I won't let you fall. Are you ready? Good. Here we go."

She pushed a button. Rick heard a humming sound. The bed was moving! Fear filled Rick again.

Slowly, the bed tipped up on its side. He was going over! Then he was over, lying on the frame she had put on his back. The bed turned till it was flat. Now he was lying on his back, with his bed on top of him.

The nurse unbuckled the straps. She took the bed off him. He could see that it was a frame just like the one which was now under him.

Now he could see more. He moved his eyes all around the room.

There were bottles hung up around him. There

were tubes going into him from these bottles.

His legs were strapped down. He couldn't move. He was helpless. But now he knew for sure that his legs were still there.

A doctor came in. It was the same doctor who had talked to him the night before. He came over to Rick and smiled down at him. "Hello," he said. "I'm Dr. Rains. How do you feel?"

"Well, Doctor, I'm scared. I'm really scared."

"Yes, I'm sure you are. You must have a lot of questions, too. What would you like to ask me?"

"What has happened to me?" Rick asked quickly. "What *will* happen to me? How long will I have to lie here?"

"OK," the doctor said. He pulled up a chair and sat down next to the bed. "Do you remember the car accident?"

"Yes. Most of it," Rick said.

"Well, your back is broken. In the backbone is your spinal cord. The spinal cord is the link from your body to your brain. And from your brain to your body. When you touch something, the spinal cord takes it to your brain. Then you can feel what you touched. When the brain tells your body something, it goes down the spinal cord. This makes your body move. Got it?"

"Yes, I think so."

"Now, your spinal cord is partly cut. This means that your brain is not in touch with the lower half of you. Everything below the place where the spinal cord is cut is out of touch. Nothing can go up. So you can't feel the lower half of you. And nothing can go down. So you can't move it."

The fear began to wash over Rick again. "And

there's nothing you can do?" he asked.

"Well, we can keep it from getting worse. That's why you have to keep still. It will heal. It will take a while. It may be months. But it will heal."

"It will heal all the way? It will fix itself?" Rick asked.

"No. Not all the way. But you may have enough of the cord left. We may find that we can teach the part that is left to do the job of the part that was cut. If we can, then you will walk again."

"And if you can't?"

"Then you'll be in a wheelchair," the doctor said. "We'll have to wait and see. Only time will tell."

Rick closed his eyes. There were those words again. He wanted to cry.

The doctor stood up. "If you have no more questions right now," he said, "I'll let your parents come in. They're waiting outside."

"OK," Rick said. "No, wait. Just one more thing."

"Yes?"

"What's with this bed? Why did the nurse turn me over?"

The doctor smiled. "Your body isn't meant to lie still. It is meant to move around," he said. "It would be hurt by lying in one place all the time. This bed will keep that from happening." He patted the metal frame. "It sure is better than a body cast."

"Yes. Sure." Rick closed his eyes. He felt very tired.

The doctor went to the door. "All right, Mr. and Mrs. Tardif. You may come in now. But just for a minute."

Rick's parents came in. They tried to smile. They

tried to look at him and not at all the tubes and straps. But Rick could see how upset they were.

"We talked to the doctor," his father said. "He said that the men from the ambulance did a really good job. He said that it could have been a lot worse. They didn't move you at all, and...."

"Yes, all right, Dad," Rick said. He didn't want to hear about it. He wished that he could turn away. But all he could do was close his eyes.

His mother touched his face very softly. "You go to sleep now, dear," she said. "We'll be in to see you later." Rick didn't open his eyes. After a minute, his parents walked quietly out of the room.

Go to sleep now. That was all he could do. Lie there and go to sleep. What a life!

He woke up when the nurse came in. She put on the other part of the bed. Then she turned him over and took off the top part of the bed. "Would you like me to turn on the TV?" she asked. "You can watch it in the mirror."

"OK," Rick said.

He watched the TV till the nurse came back. She turned him over again. "It's time for lunch," she told him. "What would you like to eat?"

Rick thought about eating. The nurse would have to feed him! Just like a baby! "I don't want anything," he said. He lay there with his eyes shut.

The day went slowly by. His parents came back again. They talked to him for a while, but he didn't feel like talking. The nurse turned him over. He watched TV. A new nurse turned him over. She fed him his supper.

At last it was night. The nurse came in with a pill.

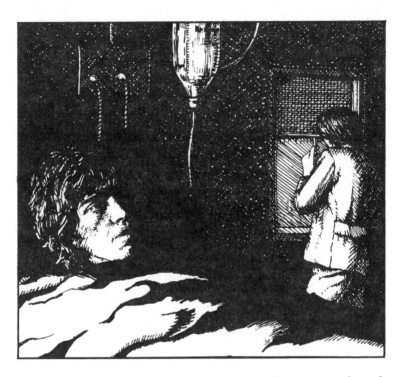

She tried to get him to take it. But he got mad and wouldn't take the pill.

So the night was just like the day. Every hour, the nurse came in and turned him over. Then, sometimes, he slept. Sometimes he just lay there.

It was the middle of the night. Everything was quiet. Suddenly, Rick heard a sound. There was someone in the room with him. "That nurse again," he thought to himself. But he didn't open his eyes. He didn't care what she was going to do.

The person walked quietly across the room. Then the sound stopped. Did she go away? Rick asked himself. Somehow he felt that someone was still in the room. He heard nothing, but someone was there.

At last he opened his eyes. He turned them as far to the side as he could. Yes, he could see someone standing by the window. It wasn't the nurse. It was a man. He was all in white. But he didn't look old enough to be a doctor.

Rick closed his eyes again. He didn't care who the man was. He didn't care what he was doing. He didn't care about anything any more!

But soon he opened his eyes again. The man was still standing there. He was looking at his watch. Then he slowly put the window shade up. Then he pulled it down again. Up. Down. Up. Then down.

The man started to turn around. Rick didn't feel like talking to him, so he closed his eyes quickly. He heard the man come up to his bed. The man stood there for a minute. Then he walked across the room and out the door.

Rick just lay there with his eyes shut. He was waiting to be turned over again.

*　　*　　*　　*　　*

Alice rolled her wheelchair down the hall. She was coming back from seeing the new babies. She went to see them every day after lunch. There was nothing like a new little baby to cheer her up!

She was just going by an open door. Room 401— that was the room of that boy who had broken his back. A car accident, the nurse had said. He was lucky that he hadn't been killed!

She should go see him, she thought. Maybe she could cheer him up.

She rolled her wheelchair up to the door. But then she heard someone in the room. He was shouting at someone. "No! I don't want my friends to come!" he was shouting. "I don't want to see them! I don't want to see anyone!"

Now Alice could hear a woman talking. It must be the poor boy's mother, she thought. The woman was asking, "Why don't you want to see anyone? Come on, Rick. Tell me."

Alice put her hands on the wheels of her chair. She started to push herself on down the hall. But then she stopped. She wanted to hear what the boy would say.

"I . . . I don't want anyone to see me like this," he said at last.

"Why not?" a man asked. "You look fine. You're just a little tied down, that's all."

"But I'm so weak, Dad! I can't move! I can't do anything for myself. They have to take care of me like a baby! I don't want anyone to see me like this. Not Kelly! Not anyone!" The boy was shouting again.

Alice shook her head. She turned and rolled slowly down the hall. Go ahead and shout, she thought. It will hurt your parents. But you have to go through it. In a few days, maybe, you'll be ready to go on. I hope so. In a few days I'll come to see you.

Alice rolled down the hall to her room. Behind her, Rick was shouting, "I don't care! I don't care about anything! Or anyone! Tell them that I don't want to see them! I don't want to see anyone! I'll just lie here and rot! I don't care!"

*   *   *   *   *

Rick's parents slipped away from his bed. But they didn't go away. He couldn't see them, but he knew they were there.

Well, he wasn't going to talk to them. He would just lie there. He didn't care.

It was very quiet in the room. His parents must be sitting by the window. They must be waiting for him to say something. Well, let them wait, he thought.

Then he thought about the man who had been in his room. He had been standing right where his parents were sitting. What had he been looking at?

"Hey, Dad," Rick called. "What can you see from where you are?"

"What, Son?" his father asked. He sounded glad that Rick had talked again.

"What can you see from where you are?" Rick asked again. "What's out that window?"

"Rick's father looked out. "There isn't much out

there," he said. "Just a parking lot. Then some trees."

"Nothing else?"

Rick's mother looked out too. "Just some cars," she said. "Why?"

"Oh, I just wondered," Rick said.

Soon it was time for his parents to go. They said good-by. Then they walked out the door and up the hall. As they went out of the door at the end of the hall, Rick's father said, "Well, I'm glad he cares about *something*. Even if it's only what's outside his window."

Directions. Answer these questions about the chapter you have just read. Put an *x* in the box beside the best answer to each question.

1. (B) When Rick woke up on the first morning

   □ a. he felt much better.
   □ b. he didn't know where he was.
   □ c. the nurse was turning him over.
   □ d. his mother and father were standing next to him.

2. (C) Before the nurse turned him over, she

   □ a. strapped the other half of the bed on top of him.
   □ b. undid the straps on the metal frame.
   □ c. gave him a pill to make him sleep.
   □ d. put the window shade up and down three times.

3. (E) Rick's spinal cord was partly cut. This meant that

   □ a. he couldn't turn his head or smile.
   □ b. he couldn't feel or move his legs.
   □ c. the doctor had to put his body in a cast.
   □ d. the doctor was sure he would never walk again.

4. (B) A man came into Rick's room in the night. Rick closed his eyes because

☐ a. he was afraid to let the man know that he was awake.
☐ b. the light hurt his eyes.
☐ c. he didn't want to see what the man was doing.
☐ d. he didn't feel like talking to anyone.

5. (C) After the man put the window shade up and down, he

☐ a. walked right out of the room.
☐ b. stood and looked at Rick.
☐ c. looked at his watch.
☐ d. called someone on the phone.

6. (E) Rick shouted at everyone because

☐ a. he didn't like to feel helpless.
☐ b. the nurses wouldn't bring him his supper.
☐ c. he was mad at the doctors.
☐ d. he didn't want the man to come into his room.

7. (D) When Alice heard Rick shouting, she didn't go into his room. This was because

☐ a. she was afraid of him.
☐ b. she didn't like his mother and father.
☐ c. she knew that he wouldn't want to talk to her yet.
☐ d. she knew that he couldn't use a wheelchair.

8. (A) Alice said, "In a few days, Rick will be *ready to go on*." What does this mean?

   ☐ a. He will be well enough to walk again.
   ☐ b. He will get out of the hospital.
   ☐ c. He can get used to what has happened to him.
   ☐ d. He can drive his car again.

9. (A) Rick's mother and father *slipped away* from his bed. This means that they

   ☐ a. fell down
   ☐ b. went away quietly.
   ☐ c. spun around on the floor.
   ☐ d. ran off.

10. (D) Rick spent a lot of time thinking about the man who had come into his room in the night. This was because

   ☐ a. his mother and father had been talking about the man.
   ☐ b. there wasn't much else to think about.
   ☐ c. he saw the man out in the parking lot.
   ☐ d. he wanted someone to talk to at night.

Skills Used to Answer Questions

A. Recognizing Words in Context   B. Recalling Facts
C. Keeping Events in Order   D. Making Inferences
E. Understanding Main Ideas

Capital Letters for People's Titles

A *title* is a name that tells something about who you are or what you do. Titles are used before and after names. And sometimes titles are used without a person's name.

Titles Before Names

If a title comes before a person's name, begin the title with a capital letter. If a title is a short way of writing a longer word, use a period after the title. For example, here are two ways to write one title:

Doctor Hall (no period)
Dr. Hall (use a period)

Here are four everyday titles. Each one begins with a capital letter. Three of them end with periods. The four titles are underlined for you.

Mr. John Jones Miss Theresa White
Mrs. Paula Williams Ms. Jean Rogers

- Mr. tells you a person is a man.
- Mrs. tells you a woman is or was married.
- Miss tells you a woman is not married. The title Miss has no period.
- Ms. tells you a person is a woman; it does not tell you whether or not she is married.

The examples below give four names and four titles. All the words have small letters. Write each name and title on the line below the name. Use periods and capitals where they belong.

1. mr peter blake

_____

2. mrs gloria downes

_____

3. miss mary kelly

_____

4. ms sonia rojski

_____

Titles Without Names

Sometimes a person's title is used without the person's name. Begin the title with a capital letter only if the title belongs to a high government official or another very important person. For example:

The President of the United States
The Prime Minister of Canada
Did the President sign the highway bill?
Will the Prime Minister speak to reporters?

Do not capitalize a title without a person's name if the person is not a high government official. For example:

The president of our class announced the dance.
The vice president of the company spoke about wages.

Exercise 2

The exercise below gives you titles without the names of the people who have the titles. Read each sentence. Look at the two ways to write each title. Then circle the correct way. The first one has been marked for you.

1. He was $\begin{bmatrix} \text{president} \\ \text{\textcircled{President}} \end{bmatrix}$ of the country during the Great Depression.

2. She was $\begin{bmatrix} \text{president} \\ \text{President} \end{bmatrix}$ of the book club last year.

3. She was the new country's first $\begin{bmatrix} \text{vice president} \\ \text{Vice President} \end{bmatrix}$.

4. He was $\begin{bmatrix} \text{vice president} \\ \text{Vice President} \end{bmatrix}$ of his high school class.

Sometimes a title is given after a person's name. The rule is the same as the rule you just learned for titles without names. Use a capital letter to begin the title only if the person is a high government official or another very important person. In the examples below, the titles are underlined.

> Dwight Eisenhower, <u>President</u> of the United States
>   (This title begins with a capital letter.)
> Don England, <u>president</u> of the bowling league
>   (This title does not begin with a capital letter.)

Exercise 3

The exercise below gives you titles that come after people's names. Read each group of words. Look at the two ways to write each title. Then circle the correct way. The first one has been marked for you.

1. Ted Loring, $\begin{bmatrix} \text{representative} \\ \text{Representative} \end{bmatrix}$ of the oil company

2. Thelma Lewis, $\begin{bmatrix} \text{representative} \\ \text{Representative} \end{bmatrix}$ of East Hurley in

    Congress

3. Kathryn Springfield, $\begin{bmatrix} \text{treasurer} \\ \text{Treasurer} \end{bmatrix}$ of the United

    States

4. Ken Sommers, $\begin{bmatrix} \text{treasurer} \\ \text{Treasurer} \end{bmatrix}$ of the Hadley Garden Club

5. Ann Johnson, $\begin{bmatrix} \text{postmaster} \\ \text{Postmaster} \end{bmatrix}$ of the United States

6. Albert James, $\begin{bmatrix} \text{postmaster} \\ \text{Postmaster} \end{bmatrix}$ of Southboro

Reading Food Ads

Your newspaper can help you save money on food. The Wednesday paper usually has a special section that tells about food. The food pages have advertisements or ads from food stores. These ads tell you what foods are on sale this week.

When a food is on sale, it costs less than it usually does. You can save money if you buy a food when it is on sale. You can save more money if you buy enough food for two or three weeks at the sale price.

Of course you should only buy foods you know you will eat. And you need a place to keep the food until you eat it. Canned vegetables are easy to keep for a long time. The ad below is for a sale of canned vegetables.

(1) SOZIO'S SUPERMARKET

(2) Sale prices good through Saturday, January 2, 1995.
(3) We have the right to limit quantities.

(4) **Corn** (8) Cream Style or Whole Kernel

(5) **4** (6) 16 ounce cans (7) **$1**

The ad gives you important information about the store and the sale. It also tells you about the foods. We have put in numbers to help you find information in the ad.

1. Look at number 1. It tells you the name of the store. Write the name on the line below. Print your answer.

_____

2. Look at number 2. It says: "Sale prices good through Saturday, January 2, 1995" This means the sale will last only until the store closes on Saturday, January 2.

3. Look at number 3. It says: "We have the right to limit quantities." This means the store can stop a person from buying all of one food. The store can make sure that some of each food is left for all the other shoppers.

4. Look at number 4. It tells you that corn is on sale.

5. Number 5 tells you how many cans of corn you can buy for the sale price. Write the number of cans on the line below.

_____ cans

6. Number 6 tells you the weight of each can. What is the number of ounces each can weighs? Write the number on the line below.

_____ ounces

7. Number 7 tells you the price for the number of cans listed in the advertisement. Write the price on the line below.

   a. _____

   Now test your arithmetic. How much does one can of corn cost? Write that amount on the line below.

   b. _____

8. Sometimes two kinds of a food will be on sale for the same price. This lets you pick the kind you like better. Number 8 tells you that two kinds of corn are on sale. Write the names of both kinds of corn on the lines below:

   a. _____

   b. _____

Using Food Ads

Here are three important things to look for when you read a food advertisement or ad:

1. what food is on sale
2. how much of the food is on sale
3. how much it costs

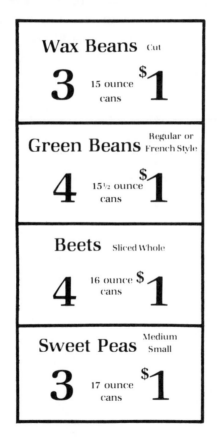

The ad on the other page is the rest of the ad for canned vegetables from Sozio's Supermarket. Look in the ad for the answers to the questions. Print your answers on the lines following the questions.

1. Look at the ad for green beans.
   How many cans of green beans are in the ad?

   _____

   How much does each can of green beans weigh?

   _____ounces

   How much do the cans of green beans cost?

   _____

   What two types of green beans are on sale?

   _____

   _____

2. Look at the ad for sweet peas.
   How many cans of sweet peas are in the ad?

   _____

   How much does each can of sweet peas weigh?

   _____ounces

   How much do the cans of sweet peas cost?

   _____

Circle the right answer: What size are the sweet peas?

Very Small   Medium Large   Medium Small

3. Look at the ad for wax beans.
    How many cans of wax beans are in the ad?

    _____

    How much does each can of wax beans weigh?

    _____ounces

    How much do the cans of wax beans cost?

    _____

    What word tells you the wax beans are not whole?

    _____

4. Look at the ad for beets.
    How many cans of beets are in the ad?

    _____

    How much does each can of beets weigh?

    _____ounces

    How much do the cans of beets cost?

    _____

What word in the ad tells you that the beets have been cut for you?

_____

5. Which vegetables cost $1 for four cans? Write the names in the order they appear in the ad.

_____

_____

How much do the cans of beets cost?

_____

If four cans cost $1, how much does one can cost?

_____

6. Which vegetables cost $1 for three cans? Write the names in the order they appear in the ad.

_____

_____

If three cans cost $1, how much does one can cost?

_____

3

On Watch

Study the words in the box. Then read the sentences below with your teacher. Look carefully at the words with lines under them.

age	cute	least	shift
booth	dragged	matter	signal
breathe	easy	money	storeroom
buzzer	forever	month	yesterday
cheerfully	hurried	never	yourself

1. He pushed the buzzer for the nurse.
2. The nurse hurried into the room.
3. It must be a signal to someone in the parking lot.
4. The day dragged by.
5. Today was a little better than yesterday.
6. It didn't matter how nice the hospital was.
7. At least it was something to think about.
8. He would never find out what the man was doing.
9. She was talking to him cheerfully.
10. He's on the night shift.
11. I think he's kind of cute.
12. He has worked here for a month or two.
13. He stepped into a phone booth.
14. He put some money into the phone.
15. We can't wait forever.
16. They're going to check the storeroom next week.
17. He hardly dared to breathe.
18. He was about Ed's age.
19. In the new bed, you can turn yourself over.
20. He has always been so easy to get along with.

Another day went by. The nurses came in and turned Rick over. They fed him and washed him. His parents came in and talked to him.

Then it was night again. He slept for a little while. Then he lay awake.

He couldn't sleep. But he wouldn't take his sleeping pill. He felt as if he was waiting for something. What was it? Just the nurse? No, it was something else. He lay awake and thought about it.

At last he had it. That man! He wanted to see if that man would come back. He had been only half awake last night. Tonight he wanted to stay awake and watch.

Hours went by. The nurses came and went. But no one else came in. Rick fell asleep.

Suddenly he woke up. Someone was in the room! He opened his eyes carefully, just a little. Yes, it was that man again.

Rick watched him. He saw the man look out into the parking lot. The man looked at his watch. Then he put the window shade up and down three times. Then he hurried out of the room.

Quickly, Rick tried to look at his clock. But he couldn't turn his eyes far enough. He waited till he thought that five minutes had gone by. Then he pushed the buzzer for the nurse.

The nurse hurried into the room. "What can I do for you?" she asked.

"I just want to know what time it is," Rick said.
The nurse looked at her watch. "It's 3:20," she

said. "Are you all right? You can't sleep? You really should take your sleeping pill, you know."

"I'm all right," Rick said. "Thank you."

The nurse checked his bed. Then she went out. Rick was left alone to think.

It was 3:20 when the nurse came in. So it had been about 3:15 when the man had been in the room.

What was the man up to? What was he doing with that window shade? It must have been a signal to someone out in the parking lot. What was going on?

Rick lay there in the dark thinking about it. It was good to have something new to think about!

*   *   *   *   *

Morning came.

The day dragged by.

In some ways, today was a little better than yesterday. The nurses didn't have to turn him over so often now. Now he could sleep better. He could hold his arms up a little bit. Now he could read the letters and get-well cards from his friends.

Things were better. But Rick felt worse. It didn't matter how nice the hospital was, he thought. It was still a hospital. And he would always be in it.

The doctor wanted him to hope for the best. But he knew. He knew that he would never walk again.

There was nothing for him to do all day. So he waited for the nighttime. Then he could wait to see if that man would come in. At least it was something to think about.

Night came. Rick got the nurse to put the clock where he could see it. He waited.

It was 2:00. 2:30. 2:45. The time dragged by. 3:00. 3:10. At last it was 3:15.

He waited.

No one came.

Rick lay there in the dark. He felt worse than ever.

*   *   *   *   *

Another day went slowly by. At last it was night. Rick watched for the man.

But he didn't come.

Another day went by. And another night. Still the man didn't come.

Where had the man gone? He must have been sent to another part of the hospital, Rick thought. Now Rick would never find out what the man had been doing.

Why were there so many *nevers* in his life?

Another morning went by.

Then, after lunch, a nurse was giving him a bath. She was talking to him cheerfully. Rick didn't feel like talking. He just lay there, looking at nothing.

Suddenly he heard something. There was someone

else in the room. He turned his eyes quickly. It was him! It was the man he had seen looking out the window. But he wasn't looking out the window now. He was just washing the floor. He didn't even look up. Soon he was done. He picked up his mop and pail and went out of the room.

"Who was that?" Rick asked the nurse.

"Who?"

"The man who was just in here. Washing the floor."

"Oh, him," the nurse said. "I think his name is Ed. He cleans the rooms."

"What kind of a guy is he?" Rick asked.

"I don't know him very well. He's on the night shift. He's just filling in on the day shift. Someone is out sick this week." The nurse looked out the open door. "I think he's kind of cute," she said, smiling.

"How long has he worked here?"

"He's new. He has worked here for a month or two, I think. But why are you asking all these questions?"

"I just wanted to know. That's all," Rick said. "Don't tell him I was asking about him."

"I won't tell him," the nurse said. "But why do you want to know about him? You're so quiet all the time. And now suddenly you're talking!"

Rick didn't say anything.

After the nurse left, he lay there and thought about the man. Ed. A new guy. The nurse thought he was cute. Sometimes he looked out of windows.

That wasn't much to go on. Rick didn't even really know what Ed's face looked like. But he would know that back anywhere. At least now he knew why Ed hadn't been around at night.

But what was Ed up to? Rick thought and thought about it. But he couldn't think of anything. He would have to wait till Ed came back on the night shift.

He gave up thinking about Ed and thought about supper.

*   *   *   *   *

Ed walked down the front hall of the hospital. He stepped into a phone booth. He looked around carefully. Then he put some money into the phone. Quickly, he put a call through.

"Hello? Steve?" he said into the phone. "This is Ed. I just found out when I'll be working next week."

"Will it be nights again? Is that guy coming back?" asked the man at the other end of the line.

"No, he's still out sick. He'll be out for a few more weeks. So I'll still be on the day shift."

"Rats! We can't wait forever. They're going to check the storeroom at the end of next week. When they see how much is gone.... They'll change the locks. And they'll watch it more carefully. That will be the end of this job. So if we're going to get any more out, it will have to be right away."

"What are we going to do?" Ed asked.

"Can't you stay on? Can't you hide somewhere till it's time?" Steve asked.

"But what if someone sees me? They'll ask questions! They'll...."

"Oh, all right! I'll do it myself!" Steve snapped.

"But... but you're on days, too! What if someone sees *you*?" Ed asked.

"I'll have to risk it, won't I? You're afraid of everything! I don't want you on the inside any more! If something went wrong, you'd be afraid to shoot! You

can do the pick-up."

"But, Steve...."

"You be there tonight! I'll give you the signal when it's clear."

"OK." Ed hung up the phone. He stepped out of the phone booth. Then he picked up his mop and pail and walked off down the hall.

* * * * *

Rick woke up suddenly. It was night. It was dark out, but the room was lit by the soft glow of the night light.

There was someone in the room with him.

It was a man. And he was walking slowly up to Rick's bed.

Suddenly Rick was afraid. What was Ed up to? What if the nurse had told him that Rick was asking questions about him? What would he do? Rick had never felt so helpless. He was all strapped down. If Ed came after him . . . .

Rick didn't move. He hardly dared to breathe. A minute went by. Then another minute.

Nothing happened.

At last he opened his eyes. He looked at the window. The man was standing there. He was looking out into the parking lot. Just as Ed had done.

But it wasn't Ed.

It was another man, taller than Ed, and thinner. He was about Ed's age, Rick thought. He was looking out the window, waiting for something.

Minute after minute went by. The man stood still, waiting. Rick lay still, watching.

Suddenly the man put out his hand. He put the window shade up. Then he put it down again. Up again. Down.

Rick watched him pull the shade. Ed had done it three times. It had to be a signal. Rick waited for the man to pull the shade up again.

Suddenly the man turned around. He looked right at Rick.

Rick's eyes were still open! He didn't move. He didn't even breathe. Could the man see his face? Did he know that Rick was awake?

If he did, what would he do?

Rick waited. It seemed like hours. But then the

man turned back to the window. He put the shade up and down again. Then he walked out of the room.

Rick waited a few more minutes before he dared to move. Then he looked at his clock. It was only 2:45. Then the time didn't matter?

He thought about the new man. So there were two guys on the inside. How many more were out in the parking lot?

Now that the man was gone, he wasn't scared any more. Being a little scared just made it all more fun. But he needed to find out more.

How could he do that, lying here in bed? Who could help him? If he asked the nurses, they might tell Ed and the other guy. Who...?

There were so many questions. There was so much to think about. But he didn't want to use it all up by thinking about it at night. He would think about it in the morning.

As he went back to sleep, he was almost happy.

* * * * *

The next morning, Rick's parents came in. "We've been talking to the doctor," they said.

"What now?" Rick asked. But just then the doctor walked in. He patted Rick's arm and smiled.

"Well, Rick," he said, "today you'll get to see something new. We're going to move you."

"What?"

"Yes, you're coming along very well. So we're going to put you in a new bed. You'll like it. In the new bed, you can turn yourself over. You just push a button. You won't have to wait for a nurse. You can turn any time you want to. So we'll just move you to Room 408, where the new bed is."

"No!" Rick shouted. "I don't want to be moved!" He had to think fast. If they moved him to a new room, then he couldn't watch Ed and the other man. He would never find out what the two men were doing. But how could he keep the doctor from moving him? He couldn't think of anything to say. So he just kept shouting, "No! I don't want to be moved! I don't want to be moved!"

"Oh, Doctor!" he could hear his mother saying. "I'm so sorry about this. I don't know what has come over him. He has always been so easy to get along with!" But Rick didn't care. He kept on shouting. It felt good.

"Don't worry, Mrs. Tardif," the doctor said. "This happens all the time. He has been through a lot." He came back to Rick's bed. "Now, Rick, what would you say if we moved the new bed in here? You are ready for this new bed. I want you to move into it. But you can stay in Room 401. All right?"

"Oh, all right," Rick said. He didn't care what they did to him. As long as he could watch for Ed.

Directions. Answer these questions about the chapter you have just read. Put an *x* in the box beside the best answer to each question.

1. (E) Ed put the window shade up and down because
   - ☐ a. the light was in Rick's eyes.
   - ☐ b. it was a signal for someone in parking lot.
   - ☐ c. it was a signal for a nurse in the hall.
   - ☐ d. Rick wanted to see what was happening.

2. (C) What did Rick do after he saw Ed come into his room the second time?
   - ☐ a. He asked his father what was outside the window.
   - ☐ b. He called the nurse and asked what time it was.
   - ☐ c. He called the nurse to turn his bed over.
   - ☐ d. He closed his eyes and went right to sleep.

3. (A) When Rick was in the turning bed, *the days dragged by*. What does this mean?
   - ☐ a. Time passed very slowly.
   - ☐ b. The sun didn't go down on time.
   - ☐ c. The bed pulled on Rick all day.
   - ☐ d. The days seemed very short.

4. (D) Rick believed that he would never walk again. Why?

☐ a. He had given up all hope.
☐ b. He had heard the nurses talking about him.
☐ c. The doctors had told him.
☐ d. His back was getting worse.

5. (D) Rick saw Ed come into his room two times. Then he didn't see Ed again. Why not?

☐ a. Ed had found out that Rick was watching him.
☐ b. Ed didn't work at the hospital any more.
☐ c. Ed was working in the daytime now, not the night.
☐ d. The rooms were cleaned by the nurse now, not Ed.

6. (B) Rick found out Ed's name by

☐ a. asking him.
☐ b. asking a nurse.
☐ c. looking out the window.
☐ d. looking it up in the phone book.

7. (B) One night a second man, Steve, came into Rick's room. Why didn't Ed come?

☐ a. He was out sick that night.
☐ b. He didn't want to give the signal any more.
☐ c. He was afraid that Rick would wake up.
☐ d. He was afraid to be seen in the hospital at night.

8. (C) Steve came into Rick's room and put the window shade up and down two times. What happened next?

☐ a. He turned around and looked at Rick.
☐ b. He stopped and looked at his watch.
☐ c. The nurse came in.
☐ d. He walked out of the room.

9. (E) After he saw Steve in his room, Rick felt almost happy. Why?

☐ a. He hoped that he could make friends with both of the men.
☐ b. It was good to have someone to talk to besides the nurses.
☐ c. He was glad that he had someone new to take care of him.
☐ d. It was good for him to have something to think about besides himself.

10. (A) The doctor said, "Rick *has been through a lot*." What does this mean?

☐ a. He has walked through a lot of doors.
☐ b. Many bad things have happened to him.
☐ c. He has been looking out the window.
☐ d. He knows a lot.

Skills Used to Answer Questions

A. Recognizing Words in Context   B. Recalling Facts
C. Keeping Events in Order   D. Making Inferences
E. Understanding Main Ideas

Capital Letters in Addresses

Use a capital letter for each word in an address. Here is a sample address:

> 123 Hope Street
> Dayton, Ohio 45404

It begins with a building number—123. And it ends with a zip code number—45404. All the words between the numbers begin with capital letters.

Street Names

The name of the street in this address is <u>H</u>ope <u>S</u>treet. Hope and Street both begin with capital letters.

There are many words for street. Here are four of them:

> avenue   road   way   drive

Here are the four words as they would look in an address. Notice that the words and the names that go with them begin with capital letters:

> <u>P</u>erry <u>A</u>venue   <u>F</u>ordham <u>R</u>oad
> <u>D</u>ouglas <u>W</u>ay   <u>B</u>rook <u>D</u>rive

Exercise 1

This exercise gives you parts of five addresses. Read each address and find the name of the street. Underline the name of the street. Then write the street name on the line after each address. Use a capital letter to begin each street name. The first one has been done for you.

1. 158 <u>thomas way</u>

   Thomas Way _____

2. 1900 rivera avenue

   _____

3. 1643 morton road

   _____

4. 17 longwood avenue

   _____

5. 982 window drive

   _____

Names of Cities

Names of cities always begin with capital letters. Their first letters are capitalized whether they are in an address or not. Here are four city names:

   Sacramento   Dallas   Atlanta   Detroit

Names of States

Names of states always begin with capital letters. Each of the four cities listed above is listed again below. This time it is listed with the name of the state in which it is found.

Sacramento, California   Dallas, Texas
Atlanta, Georgia   Detroit, Michigan

Exercise 2

This exercise gives the names of five cities and the states in which they are found. Underline the name of each city. Circle the name of each state. Then write both names on the lines after the names.

Begin each name with a capital letter. and write a comma (**,**) between both names on each line. The first pair of names has been done for you.

1. <u>phoenix</u>, (arizona)

    Phoenix , Arizona.

2. dover, delaware

    _____

3. madison, wisconsin

    _____

4. baltimore, maryland

    _____

5. boston, massachusetts

    _____

In the United States, state names are usually written in a short form in addresses. Two letters of the state name are used. These two letters are capitalized. And they are written without any space or comma between them. For example:

CA for California
TX for Texas
GA for Georgia

In an address you would write:

Sacramento CA
Dallas TX
Atlanta GA

(You don't need to remember these letters. The Post Office can tell you what letters to use.)

Exercise 3

Here are the names of five cities. Each city name is followed by the two letters that stand for the name of the state. Copy each name and the letters that follow it. But use capital letters to begin the names of the cities. And use capital letters for the state letters. The first one has been done for you.

1. denver co

Denver CO
_____

2. miami fl

_____

3. dayton oh

_____

4. new york ny

_____

5. chicago il

_____

Reading Supermarket Coupons

A coupon is part of a food ad. It gives you the right to buy a certain food for a lower price. Using coupons will help you save money when you buy food.

Wednesday is the day most newspapers have articles about food. Wednesday is also the day supermarkets have many ads for food. And it is the day that you can find the most food coupons from supermarkets.

You must read a food coupon carefully before you decide to use it. And you must be sure to bring the coupon with you when you go to the store. Clip the coupon out of the paper with a scissors. Then put the coupon with your shopping list.

Seven things you need to look for when you read a supermarket food coupon are:

1. the name of the supermarket selling the food

2. what food is being sold at a lower price

3. how much food you have to buy to get a lower price

4. the price of the food if you use the coupon

5. how much money you must spend on other things in the supermarket before you can use the coupon

6. which days you can use the coupon

7. the number of coupons one person can use for the same type of food

Look at the supermarket coupon. The numbers have been added to help you find the seven things you need to look for. Answer the questions. Print your answer on the lines that follow the questions.

1. The name of the supermarket selling the food is

_____ .

2. The food that is being sold at a lower price is

_____ .

3. Sometimes the coupon is for a larger amount of a food than you can use. How many containers must you buy to use this coupon?

_____

How much is in each container?

_____

4. What is the price of the food if you use the coupon?

_____

5. How much money will you have to spend on other
   purchases in the supermarket before you can use
   the coupon?

_____

6. What dates can you use the coupon? Supermarket
   coupons are only good for a short time, often just
   one week. Copy the whole line that tells you the
   dates you can use the coupon.

_____

7. How many coupons can one person use to for the
   same type of food? This limit on the amount of food
   one person can buy for a lower price lets more
   people save money.

_____

8. Now find the three words in the coupon that tell
   you to bring the coupon with you. Print those words
   on the line below.

_____

Using Supermarket Coupons

You know that you can save money by using food coupons from the supermarket. These coupons will help you if you read them carefully and use them only for foods you really need.

Look at the supermarket coupon below. Read all the words. Then answer the questions. Print your answer on the lines that follow the questions.

■ ■ ■ ■ ■ Shop and Save ■ ■ ■ ■ ■
With this coupon

Yogurt 8 ounce cups

3 for **$1**⁰⁰

With this coupon and a $5 purchase.
Good February 26–March 4, 1995.
Limit: 1 coupon to a customer

1. What is the name of the supermarket that is selling the food?

   _____

2. What food is the supermarket selling at a lower price?

   _____

3. How many containers do you have to buy to get a lower price?

   _____

   How much is in each container?

   _____

4. What will you pay for the food if you use the coupon?

   _____

5. How much money must you spend on other things before you can use the coupon?

   _____

6. What days can you use the coupon? Write the dates on the line below.

   _____

7. How many coupons can one person use for the same type of food?

   _____

8. Now find the three words that tell you to bring the coupon with you to the supermarket. Print the words on the line below.

   _____

4

Out of the Room

Study the words in the box. Then read the sentences below with your teacher. Look carefully at the words with lines under them.

bought	healing	ramps	together
brightly	painful	safely	unfolded
burst	physical	shelves	untie
carrying	picture	someday	upside-down
crazy	pizza	therapy	worth

1   All around her were <u>shelves</u> of boxes and bottles.
2. She took one more sheet and <u>unfolded</u> it.
3. She was <u>safely</u> out of the storeroom.
4. This hospital is a <u>crazy</u> place.
5. She tied two sheets <u>together</u>.
6. The nurses were trying to <u>untie</u> the sheets.
7. The nurse was <u>carrying</u> the pile of sheets.
8. He liked hanging <u>upside-down</u> in his bed.
9. Your back is <u>healing</u> well.
10. It's time to get going on <u>physical</u> therapy.
11. We will take you to the physical <u>therapy</u> room.
12. You might walk <u>someday</u>, too.
13. There were bars and <u>ramps</u> to help people walk.
14. It looked very slow and <u>painful</u>.
15. "Hello!" the woman said <u>brightly</u>.
16. At last Rick <u>burst</u> out, "I wish I were dead!"
17. Life isn't <u>worth</u> living like this.
18. I'd like to go out for a <u>pizza</u>.
19. I went out and <u>bought</u> it.
20. He tried to <u>picture</u> her rolling down the street.

The day was a quiet one. Alice was in her room. She was sitting in her wheelchair. A little girl was sitting on the bed next to her.

"Well, Ann, your father won't be back for a while. We have an hour all to ourselves. What would you like to do?" Alice asked.

"I don't know, Grandmother," the little girl said. Then she looked at Alice and smiled. "But you're thinking of something, aren't you? I can tell! You've got that look on your face!"

Alice rolled her wheelchair closer to the bed. She put her mouth up to Ann's ear. "Let's get me out of here," she said quietly.

"How?" the little girl asked.

"Just watch."

Alice rolled her wheelchair over to the door. She stuck her head out into the hall. She looked up and down. A nurse went by. She waited till the nurse was out of sight. Then she rolled quickly out into the hall.

She rolled down the hall a short way. She looked back. She could see Ann's head peeking out of her door. She rolled on.

Suddenly she stopped. She looked up and down the hall again. No nurses were in sight.

Quickly, she rolled up to a door. She opened the door and rolled her wheelchair into a little room. All around her were shelves full of boxes and bottles.

She went to the back of the room. Here the shelves had neat piles of clean sheets.

Alice reached up and grabbed at a pile of sheets.

The pile fell over and slid onto the floor. Some of the sheets fell into her lap. She picked up two more from the floor. Then she took one more and unfolded it. She put it neatly over the sheets on her lap.

She turned her wheelchair around quickly. Soon someone would need something from this room. She had to get out of there.

She peeked out the door. A nurse was coming! She was heading right for the storeroom, where Alice was hiding! How could Alice get out? The nurse would see her—and the sheets!

Suddenly the nurse stopped. She turned around. Then she went back to Alice's room. She stood talking to Ann.

Alice smiled. Ann had thought quickly. That girl was coming along fine.

She was safely out of the storeroom. And she could get by the nurse. But when the nurse saw the storeroom, with all those sheets on the floor... She would remember seeing Alice with the unfolded sheet over her lap.

Alice had to find a place to hide.

The nurse was turning around. It was now or never!

She dove through the open door into Room 401.

Rick was watching TV. Who had come into his room? He pushed the button on his bed. He turned the bed till he could see who it was.

He saw a little old lady in a wheelchair. She had something in her lap, with a sheet over it. She smiled at him. She looked as if she knew him. But he had never seen her before. Who was she?

The old lady turned her wheelchair around. She

looked out into the hall. She seemed to be waiting for something.

Rick saw a nurse go by down the hall. Then the old lady turned and winked at him. "See you later," she said. Then she was gone.

Rick turned his bed back again. This hospital is a crazy place, he thought. People keep popping in and out of my room. He went back to watching TV.

Alice got back to her room. No one had seen her. And she had the sheets.

"What are you going to do with these?" Ann asked.

"You'll see." Alice took two sheets and unfolded them. Then she tied them together. Then she took another sheet and tied it on.

"Grandmother!" Ann said. "You're making a rope!"

"That's right," Alice said. "Can you get that window open?"

"I'll try." Ann ran over to the window. She pulled up on it. At last she got it open.

"That's far enough," Alice said. She tied on another sheet. "Put these out the window. Don't let go of the end! How many more do we need?"

Ann leaned out the window. She looked down at the line of sheets. "Two more, I think," she told her grandmother. "That should do it. Then they will touch the ground."

"Good." Alice tied on two more sheets. "How is that?"

"That's it!" Ann said. "The last sheet is touching the ground."

"I'll tie this end to my bed," Alice said. "Then I

can slide right down to the ground. And I'll be on my way to . . . ."

Just then a nurse came into the room. "Alice!" she shouted. "What are you *doing*?"

Another nurse ran in. "What's going on?" she

asked. She ran to the window and looked down at the line of sheets. "Oh, Alice," was all she said.

Soon Ann's father came in. He looked at the nurses, who were trying to untie the sheets. Then he looked at Alice and smiled. "Mom," he said, "you've got to stop getting these nurses so upset."

"I know, Son. I know." Alice tried to look sad.

It was time for Ann and her father to go. As they got in their car, Ann asked, "Dad, was she really trying to get out?"

"Of course not," her father said. "She was just having a bit of fun. That's what keeps her going." He shook his head and smiled. "That mother of mine!" he said.

The nurse shut the window in Alice's room. Then she went out. The other nurse went out after her, carrying the pile of sheets. She shook her head. "That Alice!" she said.

Alice sat back in her wheelchair. She smiled. It had been a good day.

She got her pipe and lit it. Yes, it had been a good day.

*   *   *   *   *

Rick did like his new bed. He liked turning it. He liked turning it so that he was standing up, or even hanging upside-down.

But he was still strapped down tight. In the hospital.

The doctor said he was coming along. But it didn't mean he could walk. All it meant was a new bed.

So when his parents came in, he still felt sad. They tried to get him to let his friends come and see him. But he just shouted at his parents. He shouted at the nurses, too. He even shouted at the TV.

Every day, he waited for Ed to come in. But every time Ed did come, the nurse was in his room or out in the hall.

Rick couldn't find out anything new about Ed. All he could do was watch him carefully.

Rick tried to stay awake to watch for the night man, too. One time he thought he saw him going down the hall. But the man didn't come in.

Rick began to give up thinking about the two men. He gave up thinking about anything. He just watched TV or slept.

Then the doctor came to talk to Rick again. "Your back is healing well," he told him. "It's time to really get going on physical therapy. Today we're going to take you down to the physical therapy room."

"Will it make me walk again?" Rick asked.

"Well, I can't say for sure," the doctor said. "But..."

"Then I don't want to go," Rick said. He pushed the button. He turned the bed till he couldn't see the doctor any more.

"Rick," the doctor said, "I know how you feel..."

"No, you don't!" Rick said. "How could you? *You* aren't helpless! *You* aren't stuck in a hospital bed! *You* can walk!"

"But, Rick, you might walk someday, too! If you work hard at the physical therapy, maybe..."

"Maybe! Maybe! That's all you can say!" Rick shouted. "Well, forget it!" He waited for the doctor to go away.

But the doctor didn't go. He was talking again. "You *need* the therapy. You need it so that you can use a wheelchair. You want to get out of that bed, don't you?"

Rick didn't say anything.

"Well, you come and look," the doctor said. "It will do you good to get out of this room. You'll meet some new people, too. It'll do you good."

Rick didn't say a word. But when two nurses came in with a rolling bed for him, he didn't say no. He let them lift him onto the rolling bed. He let them push him out of his room and down the hall.

It *was* nice to see something new—even if it was just more of the hospital. He looked and looked at things as they went by. There were so many people! There was so much going on!

Soon they came to the physical therapy room. In the room, there were bars and ramps to help people walk. There were things for people to pull to make their arms stronger.

Rick looked all around. Everywhere he looked, there were people working hard. Nurses were helping them to stand, to move, to take a step. It looked very slow and painful.

The nurse put Rick's rolling bed next to the wall. "The doctor said to put you here. You can watch what's going on," she said. Then she went away.

Rick lay there and watched. It was nice to see things happening. It was nice just to turn his head.

But he wasn't going to do the therapy. All that work would go for nothing. He would never walk again. So why try?

Soon he saw someone coming. It was that old lady in the wheelchair—the one who had come into his room. Rick didn't feel much like talking to her. But how could he get away?

"Hello!" the woman said brightly. "You're here at last!"

Rick just looked at her.

"Well, you'll like it here," the woman went on. "You'll have to work hard. But the nurses are really good. My name is Alice Marks. What's your name?"

"Rick Tardif."

"I'm glad to meet you, Rick. I'm sure that we'll be friends."

The woman stopped and smiled at Rick. She seemed to be waiting for him to say something. At last he said, "Nice to meet you, Mrs. Marks."

"Oh, call me Alice. All my friends call me Alice."

"OK, Alice." Rick shut his eyes. It wasn't bad enough that he had to be in the hospital. He had to lie here and let this old lady talk at him, too.

When he opened his eyes again, Alice was gone. Soon the nurse came and took him back to his room.

*   *   *   *   *

The next day, a nurse took him back to the therapy room. But he still wouldn't do anything.

Alice was there. She smiled and waved at him. He just closed his eyes.

The next day it was the same thing. He wouldn't work. He wouldn't talk. He just lay there.

He was back in his room. Someone came in. Was it Ed again? Rick opened his eyes just a bit. Then he shut them again. It was Alice.

Alice rolled her wheelchair over to his bed. "I can see that you're awake, Rick," she said. "Now you're going to tell me what's on your mind. You don't do your physical therapy. You won't talk. All you do is shout at people. Now, tell me all about it."

Rick didn't say anything.

Alice waited.

At last Rick burst out, "Life isn't worth living like this! I wish I were dead! I wish I had been killed in that car crash!"

Alice looked at him quietly. "Why?" she asked.

"Why? I'll never walk again! That's why!" Rick said.

"Did your doctor tell you that?" Alice asked.

"Well, no. He said that we would have to wait and see. But I just know it! I just know that I'll be in this bed for the rest of my life. So why should I do therapy?"

"But you've got to have therapy! Then you can get into a wheelchair, like me!"

"But I'd still be stuck in this hospital, like you. I'll always have nurses pushing me around. I'll never do things for myself again. This life just isn't worth living!"

Alice was quiet. She was thinking hard. At last she asked, "What if you could do anything you wanted? What would you do right now?"

"Right now? Oh, I'd go out for a pizza. But I can't. No legs, no pizza. See?"

But Alice was smiling. "Wait here," she said. She turned her wheelchair around and went out the door.

"Wait here!" Rick said to himself. "Very funny. What else can I do?" He turned on his TV.

An hour went by. He almost forgot about Alice.

Suddenly he heard her wheelchair coming through the door. And he smelled something good!

He turned his head and looked at Alice. She had a

big smile on her face. On her lap was a big, flat box.

"A pizza!" Rick shouted. "Where did you get that?"

"I went out and bought it," Alice said.

"You went out and bought it? Just like that? What did the nurses say?"

"Oh, I didn't ask them," Alice said. "I just went right by them." She winked. "You can get away with anything if you *look* as if you know what you're doing. But that's enough talking." She rolled her chair up to Rick's bed. "Let's eat this thing. It's getting cold."

They ate the pizza. It was the best pizza Rick had ever had.

Then they talked. Alice told Rick about her son and his little girl. Rick told her about his parents and about Kelly. Then he told her about the accident. "How did you get hurt?" he asked.

Just then, a nurse came in to tell them it was time for supper. "I've got to get back to my room," Alice told Rick. "See you tomorrow."

That night, as he was going to sleep, Rick felt almost happy again. That Alice! She was something else, he thought. It would be good to see her again tomorrow.

He thought about her going out for his pizza. He tried to picture her rolling down the street in her wheelchair. Yes, she was really something.

He was just going to sleep when he thought of something. Alice! Alice could do it! Alice could help him find out more about Ed and the other man. She could get out in the hall and watch for him. Then she could tell Rick what was going on.

He was sure she would do it. He would talk to her about it tomorrow.

Now he would find out just what Ed and his pal were up to!

Comprehension Questions/Chapter 4

Directions. Answer these questions about the chapter you have just read. Put an *x* in the box beside the best answer to each question.

1. (B) What was kept in the storeroom at the hospital?

   ☐ a. Everything for the hospital
   ☐ b. Everything to fix a wheelchair
   ☐ c. Only sheets
   ☐ d. Everything but sheets

2. (A) The nurse was *heading* for the room where Alice was hiding. What does this mean?

   ☐ a. She stuck her head into the room.
   ☐ b. She was thinking about the room.
   ☐ c. She was walking to the room.
   ☐ d. She turned her head as she went by the room.

3. (D) The nurse didn't see Alice come out of the storeroom with the sheets. Why not?

   ☐ a. Ann called to the nurse and got her talking.
   ☐ b. Ann shut the door to the storeroom.
   ☐ c. Rick called to the nurse to turn his bed.
   ☐ d. The doctor asked the nurse to get Rick's X-rays.

4. (C) What happened right after Alice tied the sheets into a rope?

☐ a. She ran away from the hospital.
☐ b. She hid in Rick's room.
☐ c. The nurse came into her room.
☐ d. Her son came to get Ann.

5. (D) What did Alice's son think when Alice tied the sheets into a rope?

☐ a. He thought she should be locked up.
☐ b. He thought it was dangerous for Ann to be with her.
☐ c. He was afraid that she would get hurt.
☐ d. He thought it was all right for her to have fun.

6. (E) Rick wouldn't do his physical therapy because

☐ a. he didn't think he needed it.
☐ b. he didn't want to see Alice.
☐ c. he didn't like to work hard.
☐ d. he didn't think it would help him.

7. (C) When did Rick find out who Alice was?

☐ a. The first time he went to the therapy room
☐ b. The second time he went to the therapy room
☐ c. When she was hiding from the nurse
☐ d. When she gave him his pizza

8. (A) "Hello," Alice said *brightly*. How did she talk?

☐ a. Happily
☐ b. Softly
☐ c. Sadly
☐ d. Lightly

9. (E) Alice went out and bought a pizza

☐ a. because she hadn't had any supper.
☐ b. to show Rick that a person in a wheel-chair could do it.
☐ c. to show the nurses that they couldn't tell her what to do.
☐ d. because Rick asked for something to eat.

10. (B) What did Rick want to ask Alice to do?

☐ a. Ask the two men who they were
☐ b. Find out what the two men were do-ing
☐ c. Get him a pizza every day
☐ d. Help him with his physical therapy

Skills Used to Answer Questions

A. Recognizing Words in Context   B. Recalling Facts
C. Keeping Events in Order   D. Making Inferences
E. Understanding Main Ideas

Capital Letters for Names on a Map

Some names you will find on a map are names of bodies of water, like oceans, rivers and lakes. Other names on maps are the names of mountains and islands, countries and continents.

Bodies of Water

Use capital letters to begin the names of the five oceans. For example:

Atlantic Ocean   Pacific Ocean

Use capital letters for the names of rivers. For example:

Hudson River   St. Lawrence River

Use capital letters for the names of lakes. Sometimes the word *Lake* comes first in the name of a lake. Sometimes it comes second. But the word always begins with a capital letter. Here are two different examples:

Lake Huron   Wallum Lake

Exercise 1

Each sentence on the next page gives the name of a body of water. Underline the name of each body of water. Then write the name on the line below the sentence. Use capital letters where they are needed. The first one has been done for you.

1. Balboa named the <u>pacific ocean</u>.

   Pacific Ocean.

2. Mark Twain wrote about the mississippi river.

   _____

3. Lewis and Clark explored the columbia river.

   _____

4. The arctic ocean is far to the north.

   _____

5. Buffalo is on lake erie.

   _____

6. Canada and the United States border lake huron.

   _____

Mountains and Islands

Use capital letters for the names of mountains. Here are three examples:

Rocky Mountains

Mount Rainier

Whiteside Mount

Use capital letters for the names of islands. Here are three examples:

Staten Island

Isle of the Pines

Hawaiian Islands

Exercise 2

Read each sentence. Find the name of an island or a mountain. Underline the name. Then write the name on the line after each sentence. Use capital letters where they are needed. The first one has been done for you.

1. The <u>andes mountains</u> are in South America.

   Andes Mountains
   _____

2. The laurentian mountains are in Canada.

   _____

3. The tallest mountain in the world is mount everest.

   _____

4. The city of Victoria is on vancouver island.

   _____

5. The aleutian islands are near the Soviet Union.

   _____

6. Many people who work in New York City live on long island.

_____

Countries and Continents

Use capital letters for the names of countries and of continents. If a continent's name is two words, begin each word with a capital letter. Here are the names of two continents:

<u>A</u>frica   <u>S</u>outh <u>A</u>merica

In the continent of North America there are three countries. They are:

<u>C</u>anada   <u>U</u>nited <u>S</u>tates   <u>M</u>exico

If a country's name is two words, use capitals to begin each word.

Exercise 3

Read each sentence. Find the name of a country or of a continent. Underline the name. Then write the name on the line below the sentence. Use capital letters where they are needed. The first one has been done for you.

1. Wines and perfumes come from <u>france.</u>

France _____

2. The largest number of people live in china.

_____

3. Diamonds are found in south africa.

_____

4. Oil is produced in venezuela.

_____

5. English is spoken in australia.

_____

6. What country is south of canada?

_____

Reading Manufacturers' Food Coupons

You have learned how to save money by using food coupons from supermarkets. You also can save money by using food coupons from manufacturers. The manufacturers are the companies that make or package the foods.

Both types of coupons will help you if you read them carefully and use them to buy food you really need. And you must be sure to bring the coupons with you when you shop.

Manufacturers' coupons are usually found in the Sunday papers. They are printed on heavy paper, with bright colors. This makes them easy to find.

A manufacturer's coupon is different from a supermarket coupon in three important ways.

1. A manufacturer's coupon may be used in any store. It is not only for one supermarket.

2. A manufacturer's coupon is good for a much longer time than a supermarket coupon is. The coupon itself will tell you the last date you can use it.

3. A manufacturer's coupon tells you the money you save, not the price you pay.

We have numbered a manufacturer's coupon to show you where to find some of the information you need to use the coupon. It is on the next page.

(1) USE IN ANY STORE

(4) Save 40¢

(3) This coupon is good until August 31, 1995

(2) GENERAL PRODUCTS CORPORATION

Look at the manufacturer's coupon. Read all the words. Then answer the questions. Print your answers on the lines that follow the questions.

1. Look at the first line of the coupon. It does not name a supermarket. On the line below, print the four words that tell you that you can use this coupon in any store that sells the food. Use all capital letters, the way the coupon does.

_____

2. Sometimes a manufacturer's coupon names the manufacturer. Look at the bottom line of this coupon. What company manufactured this food? Print the answer on the line below. Use all capital letters.

_____

3. Look at the date near the bottom of the coupon. This is the last date you can use the coupon. This date will be six months to a year after the coupon is in the newspaper. What is the date? Print the answer on the line below.

_____

4. This coupon does not tell you how much you pay for the food. Instead, it tells you how much you save. It tells you how much is taken off the regular price. This information is in big print at the top of the coupon. How much money will you save if you use this coupon?

_____

Using Manufacturers' Coupons

You have learned that coupons will help you save money when you buy food. You also have learned that there are two types of coupons: supermarket coupons and manufacturers' coupons. The coupon below is a manufacturer's coupon.

Look at the coupon and answer the questions. Print your answers on the lines that follow the questions. Use capital letters for all words that have capital letters on the coupon.

1. The last four words on the bottom of the coupon tell you that this is a manufacturer's coupon. They tell you that you can use the coupon in any store. Print these words on the line below.

_____

2. What is the name of the food that the coupon tells about?

_____

3. The second sentence on the coupon tells you how you can use the coupon. It tells you that you can use the coupon to buy a can of any size or any kind. Print the sentence on the line below. Use capital letters where the coupon has capital letters.

_____

4. a. Does this coupon tell you the price of the food? Circle your answer.

        Yes   No

  b. Does this coupon tell you how much you save? Circle your answer.

        Yes   No

5. Four words on the coupon tell you how many coupons you can use. Print these words on the line below.

_____

6. What is the last date on which you can use the coupon? Copy the date on the line below.

_____

5

Down the Hall

Study the words in the box. Then read the sentences below with your teacher. Look carefully at the words with lines under them.

canes	fooling	key	surprised
closet	footsteps	missed	worried
creeps	great	mouths	hooked
dangerous	handles	stealing	loud
drugged	haven't	stole	showed

1. She reached around and pulled out two <u>canes</u>.
2. She grabbed the <u>handles</u> of the canes.
3. She <u>hooked</u> the canes in back of her wheelchair.
4. The nurse said, "That's <u>great</u>!"
5. The nurse looked <u>surprised</u>.
6. He <u>showed</u> her the canes.
7. What are you <u>worried</u> about?
8. No, they <u>haven't</u> moved him yet.
9. He's always <u>drugged</u> up at night, isn't he?
10. You care about those broken-down <u>creeps</u>.
11. They don't have legs—but they do have <u>mouths</u>.
12. The footsteps sounded very <u>loud</u>.
13. He could hear <u>footsteps</u> coming down the hall.
14. Had she <u>missed</u> it all?
15. They <u>stole</u> something!
16. There's a drug <u>closet</u> in the storeroom.
17. Those men must have a <u>key</u>.
18. But that would be <u>dangerous</u>!
19. Those guys are <u>stealing</u> drugs.
20. They aren't <u>fooling</u> around.

The next morning, Alice came back to see Rick. She rolled her wheelchair quickly through the door. She was already talking as she rolled up to Rick's bed.

"I've been thinking about you, Rick," she was saying. "We've got to get you out of that bed. You can't just go on lying there. You'll go crazy!"

"Oh, Alice!" Rick said. "Don't you start in on me too. The doctor is after me every day. My parents are after me, too. They keep telling me I need physical therapy. Well, I won't do it!"

"Hey! Don't get all worked up!" Alice said. "*I* don't care if you do physical therapy! That's up to you." She rolled her wheelchair up to Rick's head. "I just said we've got to get you out of that bed. Let you get out and see people. Without a nurse pushing you around."

"How can I do that?" Rick asked.

"Well, you know that rolling bed? The one they use to take you to the physical therapy room?"

"Yes. But I need a nurse to push that."

"No, you don't," Alice said. "Not if you have these!" She reached around in back of her wheelchair and pulled out two canes.

"Canes? Where did you get those?" Rick asked.

Alice smiled. "Let's just say I know where they keep things around here," she said. "Now watch." She grabbed the handles of the canes. She pushed down. The wheelchair rolled along the floor.

"Hey! That's great!" Rick said. "But could *I* do that? Could I do that lying down on a bed?"

"Sure you could," Alice said. "I used to do it all the time."

"When was that?" Rick asked. "When were you hurt? How long...."

"Oh, you don't want to hear about that," Alice said quickly. "Now, let's get a nurse in here. She can bring you that rolling bed." She hooked the canes in back of her wheelchair again. Then she rolled over and pushed the buzzer over Rick's bed.

The nurse came in. "What can I do for you?" she asked Rick.

Rick didn't know what to say. He looked at Alice. Alice told the nurse, "He wants a rolling bed."

"You do?" the nurse asked.

"Yes," Alice said. "He wants to be out in the hall. He's getting sick of this room."

"He is?" the nurse asked. "That's great!" She hurried out to get the rolling bed.

She came in pushing the bed. "Here you go. Let me get you onto it." She unbuckled Rick's straps. Then she lifted him onto the rolling bed.

"No, not on his back. Turn him over," Alice said.

The nurse looked surprised. But she turned Rick over and strapped him down. Then she pushed him out into the hall. "Where would you like to go?" she asked.

Rick looked at Alice. She held up her hand. "Stop here," Rick said. "This is fine."

The nurse stopped. "Now, be careful," she said. "If you fall off, you could hurt yourself badly. You could set yourself back for weeks." Rick said that he would be careful. The nurse went away.

Alice got out the canes again. She gave them to

Rick. "OK," she said. "Give it a try."

Rick let the canes down. At last they touched the floor. It seemed very far away.

He pushed. The bed rolled a little bit.

He pushed harder. The bed rolled again.

He pushed and pushed. The bed rolled along the floor. He was moving! By himself!

He pushed some more. But now he was getting tired. He hadn't worked so hard in a long time.

"You'd better stop now. You don't want to do too much the first day," Alice said. "I'll get a nurse to get you back to your room."

When she saw Rick, the nurse was surprised.

"How did you get all the way down here?" she asked. Rick showed her the canes.

The nurse pushed him back to his room. She lifted him back onto his bed and strapped him down.

The nurse pushed Alice out into the hall. Then she bent down and gave Alice a hug. "You're really something, Alice," she said. "You got him going when no one else could. How did you do it?"

Alice just smiled. She looked back into Rick's room. Then she rolled away.

Rick was already asleep.

*   *   *   *   *

The phone rang. Steve picked it up.

"Hello, Steve? This is Ed. Are we on for tonight?"

"I don't know. I'm getting worried."

"What are you worried about?" Ed asked.

"That guy ... The one with the broken back. Have they moved him out of 401 yet?"

"No, they haven't," Ed said. "So what? He's always drugged up at night, isn't he?"

"Yes, I think so. But.... It's funny to have the same guy in that room for so long. I may have to...."

"Take it easy on him!" Ed said quickly.

"Take it easy! You care more about those broken-down creeps than you do about us! Maybe they don't have any legs—but they do have mouths! It's a good thing I'm on tonight. If I think that guy is on to us ... I'll fix him good!"

"But...." Ed started to say.

"But nothing!" Steve snapped. "We're running out of time. I'll give you the signal tonight. Be there."

*   *   *   *   *

After supper, Alice came back to see Rick. "How

are you feeling?" she asked.

"I'm tired. My arms hurt a little. But I feel great! I want to try that rolling bed again tomorrow. I'll bet I can do more each day."

Alice smiled. "I'll bet you can, too," she said.

Rick waved a hand. "Come over here," he said. "Come up close. There's something I've been wanting to ask you to do for me."

Alice rolled her wheelchair close to Rick's bed. "What's up?" she asked.

Rick told her about Ed and the other man. He told her what he had seen. He told her about the signal with the window shade.

"They *must* be up to something!" Rick told her. "What is it? I just have to know!"

Alice leaned closer. "Where do I come in?" she asked.

"Well, you seem to know your way around this hospital," Rick said.

Alice smiled. "You might say that."

"And you can get around. So I thought you might stay up and watch for them," Rick went on. "You could watch out the window of your room. You could see what is going on out there. Then we would know what the signal is for."

"Sometime around 3:00? I'll be watching!" Alice said.

"I hope they come tonight," Rick said.

"I hope so, too," Alice said. "This could be more fun than the sheets."

"What sheets?" Rick asked. But Alice just smiled.

* * * * *

Rick lay in the dark. He lay very, very still.

Would they come tonight?

What time was it? He wished that he could look at his clock. But he didn't dare to move. He didn't want to scare them away.

Someone came down the hall. Was it Ed? No, the person walked on, by Rick's door.

The time went by slowly. It must be 3:00 by now. Was Alice still awake? Would they come tonight?

Someone walked by in the hall again. The footsteps sounded very loud. Then everything was quiet.

More time went by. They weren't coming! Rick felt like shouting in the dark. He would *never* know what the signal was for.

Suddenly, his door began to open.

Rick shut his eyes tightly. He was careful to breathe as if he were asleep. He didn't want to scare them away now!

He could hear someone walk softly into the room. He felt someone standing over him. Who was it? Was it Ed? Or the other man? Or someone else? He didn't dare to move. It was almost hard to breathe.

The man stood over him for a long time.

Why was he standing there? Did he know that Rick was awake?

What would he do if he found out?

Rick tried not to think about it. He tried to think about his breathing. In. Out. Breathe slowly. In. Out.

At last the man turned away. Rick still didn't dare to open his eyes. But he could hear the window shade go up and down. One time. Two times. Three times. Then the man walked softly out of the room.

Rick lay in the dark, trying to hear. It was so quiet! Now he could hear footsteps. They seemed very far away. A door opened and closed. Now he could hear a rolling bed being moved. Just the sounds he heard every night in the hospital. Nothing to tell him what was going on.

Outside in the parking lot, a car started up. Quietly, it drove away. "Is that a doctor going home?" Rick asked himself. "Maybe someone had a baby. Or was it Ed? I should have told Alice what he looked like."

Where *was* Alice? Had she gone to sleep? Or was she still waiting? Had she missed it all?

Suddenly Rick heard wheels rolling down the hall. They came closer and closer. Then Alice popped into his room. "I saw them!" she told him.

"Who? What were they doing?" Rick asked.

"Two men. They stole something! They stole something out of the storeroom. They went in with a rolling bed. They came out with something on the bed. There

was a sheet over it. But it looked like a pile of little boxes."

"What do you think was in them?" Rick asked.

"Drugs! I'll bet it's drugs. There's a drug closet in the storeroom. It's always locked. Those men must have a key."

"Wow!" Rick said. "What did they do then?"

"They took the bed down in the elevator. I saw all this from my door. Then I looked out my window. I saw them put the boxes into a car. Then they got in and drove away. Someone else was driving. There must be three of them."

"But what was the signal for?" Rick asked.

"To let the ones outside know when to come in. They must know what time the nurses do things. One man must come in to make sure the hall is clear. Then he signals for someone to come and help him. I'll bet they can't take too much at one time. So they keep coming back."

Rick lay quiet for a minute. "So now I know," he said.

"Well, what are we going to do about it?" Alice asked.

"*Do*? Call the police! What else? What could *we* do about it? We can't even walk."

"Oh, don't call the police yet!" Alice said. "This is too much fun. Let's give them one more night. We don't really know what they look like. We can watch and try to really see their faces."

"But that would be dangerous!" Rick said. "If those guys are stealing drugs, they aren't fooling around! That guy who was in here tonight.... I was scared! And he thought I was asleep! No, this is a job for the police."

"Oh, come on, Rick," Alice said. "There's never anything to do in this hospital. There's never any fun."

"Fun! Alice, you could be hurt! You could be killed!" Rick said.

"Hey, I seem to remember something," Alice said. "It was just the other day. Someone told me that life wasn't worth living in a wheelchair."

"But.... But.... When I said that, I didn't mean.... I didn't mean you should go out and get yourself killed!"

"Don't worry about me!" Alice said. "I can take care of myself." She patted Rick's arm. "Now I've got to get some sleep. I've got a big night tomorrow!" She rolled out of the room.

Rick lay awake for a long time. What had he got Alice into? If anything happened to her.... Maybe they wouldn't come tomorrow night, he thought. He hoped not!

But somehow he knew they would.

Directions. Answer these questions about the chapter you have just read. Put an *x* in the box beside the best answer to each question.

1. (E) The main thing that Alice did for Rick in this chapter was to

   ☐ a. get him to let his friends come to see him.
   ☐ b. turn him over when he wanted to lie on his back.
   ☐ c. show him that he could walk if he really wanted to.
   ☐ d. get him to cheer up and start moving around again.

2. (D) Where did Alice get the canes?

   ☐ a. She had them from when she got hurt.
   ☐ b. She took them from the storeroom.
   ☐ c. She asked the nurse for them.
   ☐ d. She got them out of Rick's room.

3. (D) Why didn't Alice just get the nurses to show Rick how to use the canes?

   ☐ a. She knew that he wouldn't listen to them.
   ☐ b. She knew that they didn't care about him.
   ☐ c. They didn't know how to use the canes.
   ☐ d. The doctor wouldn't let them.

4. (C) What happened last after Rick pushed himself down the hall with the canes?

- ☐ a. He called his mother and father.
- ☐ b. He got tired.
- ☐ c. He asked the nurse to push him back.
- ☐ d. He fell asleep.

5. (B) What was Ed afraid that Steve would do?

- ☐ a. Call the police
- ☐ b. Give a bad signal
- ☐ c. Hurt Alice
- ☐ d. Hurt Rick

6. (A) Rick told Alice about the two men. She asked him, *"Where do I come in?"* What did she ask?

- ☐ a. Which door should I use?
- ☐ b. What do you want me to do about them?
- ☐ c. How can I help them?
- ☐ d. How can I get into the storeroom?

7. (E) Why were the two men in the hospital that night?

- ☐ a. They were working the night shift.
- ☐ b. They were stealing drugs from the storeroom.
- ☐ c. They were cleaning the rooms.
- ☐ d. Someone had just had a baby.

8. (C) What did the man do before he gave the signal that night?

    ☐ a. He looked at Rick for a long time.
    ☐ b. He waited for the nurse to go by.
    ☐ c. He looked for Alice.
    ☐ d. He looked out into the parking lot.

9. (B) After Alice found out what the two men were doing, what did Rick want to do?

    ☐ a. Try to stop them
    ☐ b. Find out what they looked like
    ☐ c. Call the police
    ☐ d. Tell the nurses

10. (A) Rick told Alice that it would be dangerous to watch for the two men again. He said, "If those guys are stealing drugs, they aren't *fooling around!*" What did he mean?

    ☐ a. The men might kill Alice if they saw her.
    ☐ b. The men wouldn't want to play with Ann.
    ☐ c. The men didn't like to tell stories.
    ☐ d. The men were very good at their jobs.

Skills Used to Answer Questions

A. Recognizing Words in Context   B. Recalling Facts
C. Keeping Events in Order   D. Making Inferences
E. Understanding Main Ideas

Capital Letters for Calendar Words

Calendar words are the names of the days and of the months. These words are on the calendar.

The names of the seven days of the week begin with capital letters. The sentence below gives the name of a day.

Most work weeks begin on <u>M</u>onday.

The names of the twelve months also begin with capital letters. The sentence below gives the name of a month.

Lincoln's birthday is in <u>F</u>ebruary.

Exercise 1

Look for the name of a day in each sentence. Underline the name. Then write it on the line below the sentence. Begin the name of the day with a capital letter.

1. The first day of the week is sunday.

    _____

2. Are you off next saturday?

    _____

3. Our date is this thursday.

    _____

4. My favorite shows are on wednesday.

_____

5. He came home last tuesday.

_____

Exercise 2

Look for the name of a month in each sentence. Underline the name. Then write the name on the line below the sentence. Begin the name of the month with a capital letter.

1. School ends in june.

_____

2. Memorial Day is in may.

_____

3. In february we have Valentine's Day.

_____

4. School begins again in september.

_____

5. In november we have Thanksgiving.

_____

Names of the Seasons

Do not use capital letters to begin the names of the four seasons. You can remember this by remembering that the seasons are not on the calendar.

The seasons are: winter, spring, summer and fall. Another word for fall is *autumn*.

The sentence that follows gives the name of one of the seasons. The name is circled. You can see that it does not begin with a capital letter.

September is the first month of (fall.)

Exercise 3

Each sentence gives the name of a season. The names are given two different ways. Circle the correct way. The first one has been marked for you.

1. Her birthday is in the $\begin{bmatrix} \text{(winter)} \\ \text{Winter} \end{bmatrix}$.

2. In $\begin{bmatrix} \text{autumn} \\ \text{Autumn} \end{bmatrix}$ the leaves turn brown.

3. Veteran's Day is in the $\begin{bmatrix} \text{fall} \\ \text{Fall} \end{bmatrix}$.

4. This $\begin{bmatrix} \text{spring} \\ \text{Spring} \end{bmatrix}$ we will plant flowers.

Reading Unit Price Information

If two foods have the same food value, you can save money by buying the food that costs less. Often fresh foods come in packages that weigh different amounts and have different prices. This makes it hard to decide which package is the best buy.

Usually there is a label on the package that gives you important information about the price of the food. The label tells you the total price you pay for the food. And it tells you the *unit* price of the food. The unit price lets you compare two foods so you can choose the better buy.

We have added numbers to a food package label to show you the information the label gives.

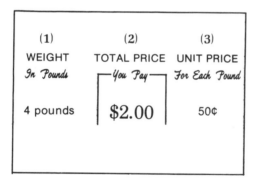

1. Number 1 tells you two things. It tells you the weight of the food. Print the weight of the food on the line below.

_____

Number 1 also tells you the *unit* of weight. A unit is a standard amount used to measure something. Some units of weight are pounds, ounces, grams and kilograms. The unit of weight for this package is the pound.

2. Number 2 tells you the total price you pay for the package of food. Print that price on the line below.

_____

Number 3 tells you the *unit price*. This price is the price for each *unit* of the food. The unit price of this food is 50¢ for each pound.

Let us see how the store figured out the unit price. We will use the information on the package label. The example below shows the arithmetic the store did.

You can see that the total price of the food was divided by the number of units of the food. The result is the unit price, the price for each unit of the food.

Example:

$$4 \overline{\smash{)}\begin{array}{l} .50 \text{ unit price} \\ \$2.00 \text{ total price} \end{array}}$$

Look at the label below. It tells you the weight of the food, the unit of weight and the total price of the food. It does not tell you the unit price. Use the information on the label and your arithmetic skills to answer the following questions. Print your answers on the lines following the questions.

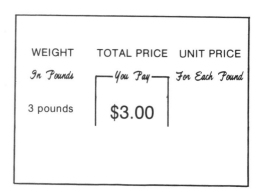

3. What is the unit of weight for this food? It is the

_____

4. What is the weight of the food?

_____

5. What is the total price of the food?

_____

6. What is the unit price of the food?

_____ for each _____

Using Unit Price Information

You have learned that using unit prices of foods can help you save money. When two foods have the same food value, the food that costs less is the better buy. It is the *unit price*, the price of one unit of the food, that lets you compare the costs of the two foods.

Sometimes the unit price of a food is given on the package or on a sign near the food. But sometimes you have to figure out the unit price for yourself. The charts that follow will give you practice in figuring out unit prices.

Chart Directions. To complete Chart 1, figure out the unit price for each food. Then print the unit price in the blank space at the right of the chart. The first unit price has been filled in for you. And the example on the next page shows you how the price was figured out.

Chart 1

Total Weight and Units of Weight	Total Price You Pay	Unit Price
1. 5 pounds	$1.00	_20¢_
2. 5 pounds	$1.50	_____
3. 5 pounds	$2.00	_____

Example:

$$5\,\overline{)\,\$1.00}\quad\begin{array}{l}.20\quad\text{unit price}\\[-0.3em]\text{total price}\end{array}$$

Often larger packages or containers of a food have lower unit prices. This makes the larger amounts better buys *if* you can use the larger amount. Chart 2 gives you total weights and total prices for larger amounts of the food listed in Chart 1.

Chart Directions. To complete Chart 2, figure out the unit price for each food. Then print the unit price in the blank space next to the total price. The example after Chart 1 will help you remember how to do the arithmetic.

Chart 2

Total Weight and Units of Weight	Total Price You Pay	Unit Price
1. 10 pounds	$10.00	_____
2. 10 pounds	$15.00	_____
3. 10 pounds	$25.00	_____

Comparing Charts

Use both charts to answer the following questions. Print your answers on the lines that follow.

1. What is the unit of weight for each package of food? It is the

   _____

2. What is the highest of all six unit prices? Print the amount of money on the line below.

   _____

3. What is the lowest of all six unit prices? This package would be the best buy *if* you need all the food in the package. Print the lowest unit price on the line below.

   _____ for each _____

6

In Front of the Gun

Study the words in the box. Then read the sentences below with your teacher. Look carefully at the words with lines under them.

against	danger	moment	third
because	downstairs	raised	trigger
believe	family	shirt	true
bullet	married	straining	unplugged
crashed	mixed	tests	upstairs

1. "Keep your <u>shirt</u> on!" Steve said.
2. At that <u>moment</u>, the men were in the parking lot.
3. The <u>third</u> man started up the car.
4. He wanted to <u>believe</u> her.
5. Rick was <u>straining</u> to hear what was going on.
6. Alice was in <u>danger</u>.
7. What a time to go <u>downstairs</u> for coffee!
8. The buzzer was <u>unplugged</u>.
9. It must be <u>true</u>!
10. "We're going <u>upstairs</u>," Steve said.
11. He <u>raised</u> his arm and pointed his gun at her.
12. He started to pull the <u>trigger</u>.
13. The bed slammed <u>against</u> the wall.
14. Rick slid off the bed and <u>crashed</u> to the floor.
15. There is a <u>bullet</u> hole in you.
16. It's all <u>because</u> of me!
17. I got you <u>mixed</u> up with them.
18. I'm in the hospital for other <u>tests</u>.
19. After you got hurt, you got <u>married</u>.
20. You had a <u>family</u> while you were in a wheelchair.

The day went by slowly.

In the morning, Rick got on the rolling bed again. He went as far as he had the day before. But he wasn't so tired.

After lunch, he tried it again. He got almost to the end of the hall. He got Alice to show him the door to the storeroom.

He was happy to be out of his room. But he kept thinking about that night. What would happen?

After supper he tried the rolling bed again. Alice showed him how to turn around. He even got through his door by himself.

The nurse lifted him back onto his bed. She strapped him down. She was going to take the rolling bed away. Just then, someone called her. She left the rolling bed next to Rick's bed and hurried out. Rick was glad. He liked to look at the rolling bed. He liked to think about getting out.

Alice came by to say good night. "Wish me luck tonight," she said.

"What are you going to do?" Rick asked her.

Alice smiled. "Oh, I'm just going to watch for our friends," she said. "Don't worry about a thing. I'll be all right."

"Be careful!" Rick said.

"Oh, I will. Good night."

*   *   *   *   *

At the other end of the hall, Ed stepped into the phone booth. He called Steve.

"Steve? This is Ed."

"Where are you? Why are you calling now?" Steve asked.

"I'm at the hospital. I couldn't call you before. That guy came back to work today. So I'm back on the night shift."

"You are? Then we'll have to go back to the old way. I don't like it. I don't like to change things on the last night. But we'll have to risk it."

"OK. I'll give the signal when it's all clear," Ed said.

"And watch that creep in 401." Steve said. "If he moves, give it to him! You've got to!"

"Yes. All right. See you later." Ed hung up the phone.

*   *   *   *   *

It was night. Most of the hospital windows were dark.

A car waited in the parking lot. Two men sat in it. They were looking up at the hospital. They were watching one window.

"What's taking him so long?" one of the men asked.

"Keep your shirt on! He's got to be sure that the hall is clear. It should be soon. Look! There it is now!"

At one window, the shade was moving. It went up. Then down. Then up again. Down. Up. Down.

"That's it. Let's go."

The two men got out of the car. One of them stood leaning against the car. The other one hurried in the back door of the hospital.

A rolling bed was waiting by the door. The man grabbed it and pushed it into the elevator.

When he came out of the elevator, another man

was waiting for him. "All set, Ed?" he asked.

"Yes, Steve. All set."

"Let's go." The men pushed the rolling bed quickly down the hall. Ed opened the door of the storeroom. Steve pushed the bed into it.

Ed unlocked the drug closet. Quickly, the men took boxes out of the closet. They piled the boxes on the bed. Then Steve took a sheet and put it over the boxes. Ed locked the closet door again.

The men were working fast. They didn't look around in the storeroom. They didn't look at the wheelchair behind the shelves.

They didn't see that there was someone in the wheelchair.

Alice was watching them carefully. She could see their faces when they piled up the boxes. She would know the men again later. The police would come, and she would tell them what the men looked like. It would be so much fun. Wait till Ann heard about *this*!

The men went out, closing the door quietly behind them. Alice waited till they had been gone for a few minutes. Then she rolled her wheelchair out from behind the shelves.

At that moment, the men were in the parking lot. The boxes were all in the car. The third man started up the car.

"Good work, Ed," Steve was saying. "I'll see that you get your cut. Now you'd better get back in there. You'd better get back to work. Someone might come looking for you."

"Right. Well, good-by."

"So long."

Steve jumped into the car. The car pulled out. Ed went back into the hospital.

In the storeroom, Alice sat near the door. She heard the car start up. Then she heard it pull out. "It's safe to come out now," she said to herself. "But I'll wait a minute more—just to be sure."

At last she opened the door to the storeroom. She rolled her wheelchair out the door.

Just then, Ed walked out of the elevator.

He looked at Alice. His mouth fell open. For a moment, he just stood there. Then he ran up to her and grabbed her wheelchair. "What were you doing in there?" he snapped.

Alice was thinking fast. "What's the matter with you?" she asked. "I didn't go in there. I just saw that the door was open. I thought I would shut it. But do you thank me for it? Oh, no. You come and yell at me for it. You hospital people are all the same." She tried to roll her wheelchair away.

Ed held onto the wheelchair. He looked at Alice. He wanted to believe her. He had heard the nurses talking about her, about the way she talked. They said she was great to have around.

But he knew that he had shut the door.

"I'll take you back to your room," he said. "You have a phone in your room, don't you? I have to call a friend of mine." He pushed the wheelchair slowly down the hall.

* * * * *

Rick was lying in the dark. He was straining to hear. What was going on? Where was Alice?

He could hear people talking out in the hall. But he couldn't hear what they were saying. What was going on?

Then he saw Alice go by his door.

And Ed was pushing her.

They had seen her! They had seen her watching them! Now they had her. She was in danger. Someone had to help her!

He grabbed for the buzzer over his head. He pulled it down and pushed it hard. Now the nurse would come. The nurse would call the police. "Oh, hurry, Nurse, hurry!" Rick said to himself.

The nurse didn't come.

Rick pushed the buzzer again and again. Where was the nurse? Why didn't she come? What a time to go downstairs for coffee!

If only he had a phone! But he had kept telling them he didn't want one.

He pushed the buzzer again. Where was that nurse? Then he thought of something. He turned his bed over and looked at the wall.

The buzzer was unplugged. When he grabbed it, he had pulled the cord right out of the wall.

Now he knew. The nurse couldn't help Alice.

It was up to him.

The rolling bed was still near him. Could he reach it? He reached out. He touched it. A little more.... His hand reached out.... A little more.... He got hold of it and pulled it to him.

Quickly, he unbuckled the straps on his bed. Now he had to get himself onto the rolling bed. He pulled hard on the bed. He began to slide. Bit by bit, he slid over to the rolling bed. He had to be careful. The nurse had told him that he would be hurt if he fell. But he had to hurry, too.

Now he was sliding from one bed to the other. The rolling bed moved a little. What if it rolled out from under him? He had to make it.

At last he was on the rolling bed. He was very tired. But he couldn't take time to rest. He grabbed the canes. He pushed the bed out into the middle of the room. Then he turned it around and headed out the door.

When he got out into the hall, he stopped. What should he do now? There was no one around. Where was the nurse? She could be in any room.

Where was the nearest phone? There must be one at the nurses' desk. But that was at the end of the hall—past Alice's room. Ed would see him.

He couldn't take time looking. He would have to go downstairs.

Rick pushed the rolling bed to the elevator. He pushed the button. The doors opened right away. He pushed the button for the first floor. The elevator moved down. The doors opened again.

Rick pushed himself out. A nurse came running up to him. "Hey! What are you doing down here?" she asked.

"Quick! Call the police!" Rick told her. "There's a killer upstairs! I'm sure he has a gun! He's going to kill Alice Marks!"

"A killer? With a gun?" the nurse asked. She smiled. "Did that Alice put you up to this?"

"No! It's true! There really is a man up there! He was stealing drugs from the storeroom. Alice saw him. So he's going to kill her!"

The nurse looked at him. "Are you sure this is for real?" she asked.

"Yes! Yes!" Rick was almost crying. "For God's sake, *hurry*! Call the police!"

But the nurse still didn't move. "I don't know," she said. "That Alice.... Wait a minute! You're the guy with the broken back! The one who won't do physical therapy!"

"It doesn't matter who I am! *Call the police*!"

"If you came all the way down here.... It must be true!" The nurse ran down the hall. Rick could see her pick up the phone. He let his head drop down onto the bed. He was so tired. Thank God it was all over.

A door opened next to him. A man stood looking at him.

It was the man who had been in his room.

And the gun in his hand was pointing right at Rick's head.

"So you *were* awake," Steve said. "I thought so." He looked down the hall at the nurse. She was talking into the phone. If only she would look around! But she didn't.

"We're going upstairs," Steve said. He held the gun closer to Rick's head. "If you call out, I'll kill you on the spot."

He pushed the button for the elevator. Soon they were moving quickly down the hall to Alice's room.

Steve pushed Rick into the room. Rick could see

Alice. Ed was pointing a gun at her. But she was still all right!

Ed looked at Rick. Then he looked at Steve. "What did you bring him in here for?" he asked.

"Well, I found him downstairs," Steve said. "He had gone for help. I *told* you we should have got rid of him before. We'll have to do it now—and quick! The police will be here soon."

Ed didn't say anything. He just looked at the floor.

"All right," Steve said. "It's all up to me. This isn't a job for Mr. Nice Guy." He gave Rick's bed a push. It rolled over next to Alice's wheelchair. Then he came slowly across the floor and stood over them.

He raised his arm. He pointed his gun at Alice's head. He started to pull the trigger.

"Hey!" Rick shouted. He threw one cane down on the floor with a crash. At the same time, he put the other cane down and pushed hard. The bed rolled across the floor and slammed against the wall so hard that it bounced back. Rick slid off the bed and crashed to the floor next to the wall.

Steve turned around fast. The gun went off with a flash.

Alice grabbed Rick's cane from the floor. Before Steve could turn back to her, she slammed the cane down on the side of his head. He fell to the floor and lay still.

Ed raised his gun. He pointed it at Alice. She looked at him quietly.

At last he put the gun down again. "I can't do it," he said.

Alice rolled her wheelchair around Rick's bed. She looked down at Rick. "Rick! Can you hear me? Are you all right?" she called.

"I can hear you," Rick said. "But I can't move."

"Don't try." Alice rolled closer to him. "Rick! You're bleeding! You've been shot!"

"Really?" Rick asked. "Where? I can't feel anything. Maybe sometimes it's a help not to feel your legs."

Just then someone ran down the hall. "Don't anyone move!" came a shout from the door.

"Don't worry," Alice called. "Everything is all right."

Two policemen came in. They took Ed's gun. Then they stood over Rick and Steve on the floor. "Don't anyone move," they said again.

"Don't worry," Rick said. "We can't."

*   *   *   *   *

The next morning, Alice was sitting by Rick's bed. Her son was standing next to her.

"I feel so bad about this!" she said. "Poor Rick! Here you are, back in the bed you were in first. You're right back where you started. With a bullet hole in you, too! And all because of me!"

"Don't worry about it, Alice!" Rick said. "I was the one who asked you to watch for those men. I was the one who got you mixed up with them. And thanks to you, they got all three of them."

"Well, thank you for going for help," Alice said. "You saved my life."

"And you saved mine! You sure hit that guy hard! How did you get to be so strong?"

"She's been pushing herself around in a wheelchair all her life," her son said. "That makes your arms strong."

"All your life?" Rick asked. "Why didn't you tell me this before?"

"I didn't think you would want to hear about it," Alice said. "I was hurt when I was a little girl. I'm in the hospital now for some other tests."

"You were hurt when you were a little girl! Then you got married! And had a family! When you were in a wheelchair!"

"She sure did," Alice's son said. "And she was the best mother a guy could have."

"How about that!" Rick said. He smiled. "So life in a wheelchair *is* worth living. But the doctor says I still might walk. And I'm sure going to give it a try! As soon as I'm ready again, I'm going to start physical therapy."

"That's great," Alice said. Then she looked around. Someone was standing by the door. Alice touched her son's arm and pointed to the door. He took hold of her chair and pushed her out of the room.

"Where are you going?" Rick called after them. "Hey! Who's there?"

A girl walked quietly into Rick's room. "Hello Rick," she said.

"Kelly!" Rick said. "What are you doing here?"

"Your nurse called me. She said that you were asking to see me."

"My nurse?" Rick thought for a moment. "Did she tell you her name?"

"Yes. She said her name was Alice."

"That Alice!" Rick said. He smiled and took Kelly's hand. "It's really good to see you, Kelly," he said.

Directions. Answer these questions about the chapter you have just read. Put an *x* in the box beside the best answer to each question.

1. (A) "Watch that creep in that room!" Steve told Ed. "If he moves, *give it to him!*" What did Steve tell Ed to do?

   ☐ a. Give Rick a gun
   ☐ b. Give Rick a sleeping pill
   ☐ c. Kill Rick
   ☐ d. Call the nurse

2. (C) Alice came out of the storeroom

   ☐ a. right after the men went out of the storeroom.
   ☐ b. right after the men came into the storeroom.
   ☐ c. as soon as she heard their car drive away.
   ☐ d. when Ed grabbed onto her wheelchair.

3. (D) Alice didn't think that Ed would come back to the hospital because

   ☐ a. she knew that he was afraid of her.
   ☐ b. she thought that the men would never come back to the hospital.
   ☐ c. she didn't know that he was working on the night shift.
   ☐ d. she didn't know that he worked at the hospital.

4. (D) Why did Ed call Steve after he saw Alice coming out of the storeroom?

☐ a. He didn't want to kill her himself.
☐ b. He knew that she was a friend of Steve's.
☐ c. He wanted Steve to see how brave he was.
☐ d. He wanted to ask him if Alice could help them.

5. (E) Rick got on the rolling bed and went for help

☐ a. just to show that he could do it.
☐ b. because there was no one else to do it.
☐ c. because he thought it would be fun.
☐ d. so that Alice wouldn't be mad at him.

6. (B) When Rick told the nurse that someone was going to kill Alice, she didn't believe him at first. What made her believe him?

☐ a. She saw Steve with a gun.
☐ b. The police came in.
☐ c. She saw that Rick had been shot.
☐ d. She remembered who Rick was.

7. (C) What happened just before Alice grabbed the cane and hit Steve over the head?

☐ a. Steve shot Rick.
☐ b. Ed yelled at Steve.
☐ c. Steve pointed his gun at Alice.
☐ d. Alice shouted, "Hey!"

8. (A) Alice said, "I feel so bad about this. Poor Rick! *You're right back where you started.*" What does this mean?

☐ a. Rick is just as weak as he was right after the car accident.

☐ b. Rick's back has started to get better.

☐ c. Rick is right that he will never walk again.

☐ d. Rick is driving on the road where he had the accident.

9. (E) How did Rick feel when he found out that Alice had been in a wheelchair for a long time

☐ a. He felt very sad for her and her family.

☐ b. He was mad at the doctors because they couldn't heal her.

☐ c. He was glad to know that a person in a wheelchair could do so much.

☐ d. He felt bad because he knew that he would never walk again.

10. (B) Who told Kelly that Rick wanted to see her?

☐ a. Rick

☐ b. Rick's mother and father

☐ c. The doctor and nurse

☐ d. Alice

Skills Used to Answer Questions

A. Recognizing Words in Context   B. Recalling Facts

C. Keeping Events in Order   D. Making Inferences

E. Understanding Main Ideas

Capital Letters for Some School Courses

Language Courses

The sentence that follows gives the name of a language course. You can see that the capital letter that begins the name is underlined.

Harold is taking Spanish this year.

Exercise 1

Look for the name of a language in each sentence. Underline the name. Then print it on the line below the sentence. Begin the name with a capital letter. The first one has been done for you.

1. All American junior high schools teach english.

   English

2. Sixty students in our high school take french.

   _____

3. The first high schools taught latin.

   _____

4. My high school teaches chinese now.

   _____

5. Helen can speak german and read it.

_____

6. Emily learned russian at home.

_____

Courses with Numbers

Use a capital letter to begin the name of a course that has a number. The number is there to tell you what year or what term the course is. The sentence below gives you a course name with a number. You can see that the capital letter at the beginning of the course name is underlined.

Marissa's first course was <u>A</u>lgebra 1.

Exercise 2

Look for the name and number of a school subject in each sentence. Circle the number. Then print the whole name on the line under the sentence. Print the name and the number. The first one has been done for you.

1. Paul studies geography ②.

   Geography 2

2. Is Carla taking biology 3 this term?

_____

3. Peter is beginning cooking 1 tomorrow.

_____

4. We have a new course, typing 5.

_____

5. Did Jack fail history 1 again?

_____

6. I hope Cheryl passes geometry 2 this year.

_____

Do *not* capitalize course names that are not languages or do not have numbers. The sentence that follows gives the name of a course. You can see that the course is not a language. You can also see that it does not have a number. For these reasons, the course name does *not* begin with a capital letter.

Agnes liked music best.

Exercise 3

Find the name of a school subject in each sentence. Each subject name is given two times. It is given first with a small letter. Then it is given with a capital letter. Circle the way that is correct. The first sentence has been marked for you.

1. Sam is studying ⎡(shorthand)⎤ .
⎣Shorthand⎦

2. Alice is beginning $\begin{bmatrix} \text{biology} \\ \text{Biology} \end{bmatrix}$.

3. Lois doesn't like $\begin{bmatrix} \text{typing} \\ \text{Typing} \end{bmatrix}$ class.

4. Roger failed $\begin{bmatrix} \text{woodworking} \\ \text{Woodworking} \end{bmatrix}$ last year.

5. Sidney got a prize in $\begin{bmatrix} \text{civics} \\ \text{Civics} \end{bmatrix}$ last term.

6. Joan likes $\begin{bmatrix} \text{history} \\ \text{History} \end{bmatrix}$ best.

Reading Nutrition Labels

Most food containers have nutrition labels that tell you about the food inside. *Nutrition* information is information about food that will keep you healthy. *Nutrients* are what is in food to make it good for people.

Look at the nutrition label below. It is from a box of cereal. We have put numbers on it to help you find what you need to know about the cereal.

NUTRITION INFORMATION
(1) (per serving)

(2) { Serving Size=1 ounce
Number of servings in this box=7

(3) Calories 110

(4) { Protein .... 4 grams
Carbohydrates .... 20 grams
Fats .... 2 grams

(5) Percentage of Each Nutrient That Is in This Box

Protein 6%
Vitamin A 25%
Vitamin B6 .... 30%
Vitamin B12 .... 28%
Iron 23%

Number 1 tells you that the nutrition information is given for one serving. A serving is how much one person will eat.

Number 2 tells you two things. It tells you the size of a serving. And it tells you the number of servings in the box.

We have printed this information below.

Size of serving __*1 ounce*__

Number of servings in this box __*7*__

This information means you can get seven breakfasts from this box.

Number 3 tells you that there are 110 calories in one serving of cereal. (This is just the dry cereal, with no milk added to it.)

Number 4 tells you about the nutrients in the cereal. The three most important nutrients are protein, carbohydrates, and fats. The amounts of these nutrients are given in *grams*, a very small unit of weight. We have printed the amounts of these nutrients below.

protein __*4 grams*__

carbohydrates __*20 grams*__

fats __*2 grams*__

You need some of each nutrient each day. The whole amount that you need is 100% of what you need. The nutrition label tells you how much of the 100% you will get from one serving of the food. For example, the cereal label tells you that a one-ounce serving of cereal will give you 6% of the protein you need today. This means you will need to get 94% of your protein from the other foods you eat today. The 6% from the cereal and the 94% from the other foods will add up to 100% of the protein you need.

Number 5 on the cereal label tells you what percentage of each nutrient is in the cereal. Two important types of nutrients are vitamins and minerals. This cereal has Vitamins A, B6, and B12. We have printed the percentages of these vitamins below.

Vitamin A _____ *25%* _____

Vitamin B6 _____ *30%* _____

Vitamin B12 _____ *28%* _____

The last line of the nutrition label tells you that one serving of the cereal will give you 23% of the iron that you need today.

You can see from the label that this cereal gives you only a small amount of the protein that you need. But you can also see that the cereal gives you larger amounts of three vitamins and of iron. The cereal is a better way to get these nutrients than to get protein.

Using Nutrition Labels

You know that nutrition labels tell you how foods help you stay healthy. They help you know what nutrients are in foods and how much of the nutrients the foods have.

Here is a nutrition label from a can of tuna. Use the label to answer the following questions. Print your answers on the lines that follow each question.

```
NUTRITION INFORMATION
         (per serving)

    (1) Serving Size=7 ounces
   (2) Number of servings in this can=1
 (3) Calories ....................... 240
 (4) Protein .................. 50 grams
     Carbohydrates ............0 grams
     Fats......................3 grams

(5) Percentage of Each Nutrient
    That Is in This Can
 Protein ......................110%
 Vitamin A ......................0%
 Vitamin B6 ...................40%
 Vitamin B12...................50%
 Iron ...........................4%
```

1. What is the size of one serving?

   _____

2. How many servings are there in this can?

   _____

3. How many calories are in each serving?

_____

4. How many grams of protein are in each serving?

_____

5. What percentage of your daily need for protein will you get from one serving?

_____

6. How many grams of carbohydrates are in each serving?

_____

7. How many grams of fat are in each serving?

_____

This can of tuna will give you some of the nutrients you need every day. Look at the list of nutrients given below. Then look again at the label to find out what percentage of each nutrient you can get from the tuna. Write each percentage on the line below the name of each nutrient.

8. Vitamin A

_____

9. Vitamin B6

_____

10. Vitamin B$_{12}$

_____

11. Iron

_____

To the Instructor

Purpose of the Series

Teachers charged with the responsibility of providing instruction for adults and older students with reading difficulties face a major problem: the lack of suitable materials. Stories written at the appropriate level of maturity are too difficult; stories easy enough to read independently are too childish.

The stories in the Adult Learner Series were written to solve the readability problem. The plots and characters in these stories are suitable for adults and older students, yet the stories can be read easily by very low-level readers.

The principal goal of the series is to provide interest and enjoyment for these readers. To this end, every attempt has been made to create a pleasant reading experience and to avoid frustration. The plots move quickly but are kept simple; a few characters are introduced and developed slowly; the same characters are utilized throughout a text; sentence structure and vocabulary are carefully monitored.

A secondary goal is to help adults explore and develop everyday life skills. Lessons and exercises about a variety of life skills provide adults and older students with the basic competencies they need for success in this fast-paced world.

Rounding out the structure of the series are exercises for developing vocabulary skills, comprehension skills, and language skills.

Reading Level

The stories in the Adult Learner Series are all written at second grade reading level. It should be kept in mind, however, that the stories were written for adults: people with a wider range of experience and larger speaking and listening vocabularies than those of elementary school children. Thus, there are some words and some events which might present difficulties for elementary school students but which should not pose problems for older beginning readers.

Besides the slightly increased complexity of vocabulary and plot, the writing style itself has been adapted for older beginning readers. Every effort was made to make the prose sound natural while maintaining simplicity of structure and vocabulary. The repetition of words and phrases has been carefully controlled to permit maximum learning of new words without producing a childish effect.

The reading level of the stories was established by the use of the *Fry Readability Formula*. According to this formula, the range of reading levels of the chapters of this book is from grade 1.4 to 1.8.

Ninety-two percent of the words used in *The Secret of Room 401* are included in *3,000 Instant Words* by Elizabeth Sakiey and Edward Fry; 88 percent are among the first 2,000 words in that book, which lists the 3,000 most common words in the English language, ranked in order of frequency. The first 100 words on the list and their common variants [*-s, -ing*, etc.] make up 50 percent of all written material. The first 300 words and their variants make up 65 percent of all written material. Because readers encounter a relatively small number of words so frequently, they must be able to recognize the Instant Words immediately to be effective readers.

The story line of *The Secret of Room 401* provides a range of vocabulary words that the student may find very necessary on some occasions in his or her own life: words like hospital, ambulance and emergency room.

The length of some of these words may give the student some difficulty at first, so the instructor may wish to provide some assistance during the reading of the first chapter. However, the words will soon become familiar, and the subsequent chapters should present few if any problems in vocabulary. Students will need more help with the exercises.

Structure and Use of the Text

Each book in the Adult Learner Series is divided into several units. Each unit follows a regular format consisting of these sections:

Preview Words

Twenty words from each chapter are presented for students to preview before reading. Those words that were expected to give students the most difficulty were chosen for previewing. The preview section includes all words of more than one syllable that are not among the first 2,000 words on Sakiey and Fry's list of 3,000 Instant Words. The words are listed first in alphabetical order and then shown again in story sequence in sentences based on each chapter.

The twenty sentences match the chapter in readability; students can read the sentences independently. With some classes the instructor may want to read the words and sentences aloud for students to repeat and learn. In very structured classes, the words could also be used for spelling and writing practice.

Story

The primary purpose of the story is to provide interesting material for adult readers. It should be read as a story; the element of pleasure should be present. Because of the second grade reading level, students should be able to read the story on their own.

The first page of each chapter has a gray band at the top. This makes it easy to find the story pages. Students should be encouraged to return to these pages often and to reread the stories.

Comprehension Questions

Ten multiple-choice comprehension questions follow each chapter. There are two questions for each of these five comprehension skills:

A. Recognizing Words in Context
B. Recalling Facts
C. Keeping Events in Order
D. Making Inferences
E. Understanding Main Ideas

The letters *A* through *E* appear in the text as labels to identify the questions.

The comprehension questions are constructed to cover all parts of the chapter evenly and to bring out important points in the story. This insures that the student understands the story so far before going on to the next chapter.

Students should answer the questions immediately after reading the chapter and correct their answers using the key at the back of the book. Students should circle incorrect responses and check off the correct ones.

The graphs at the back of the book help the instructor keep track of each student's comprehension progress. The *Comprehension Progress Graph* shows comprehension percentage scores. The *Skills Profile Graph* identifies areas of comprehension weakness needing special attention and extra practice.

Language Skills

These sections cover many aspects of language study: phonics, word attack skills, simple grammar, and correct usage. The readability of these sections is higher than that of the chapters. The readability level varies depending on the vocabulary load of the specific language skill being taught.

Because the language skills are taught in clear and simple terms, most students will be able to work these sections independently. However, the instructor should be alert for opportunities to explain and further illustrate the content of the lessons.

The lessons contain exercises which give students the opportunity to practice the language skills being taught. An answer key at the back of the book makes it possible for students to correct their work.

Understanding Life Skills

Every chapter is accompanied by two sections which deal with life skills. The first, "Understanding Life Skills," introduces and fully explains a specific life skill. The life skills all revolve around some detail of modern adult life.

Because this section stresses *understanding* a

certain life skill, the reading level is higher than the reading level of the story. However, the life skill lessons are presented in carefully prepared steps, and most students should be able to read and comprehend them without too much difficulty.

Questions used in the lessons are designed to focus the students' attention and to reinforce the learning. Answers for all questions are provided at the back of the book.

Applying Life Skills

Because modern-day living requires both *knowing* and *doing*, two life skills sections follow each chapter to emphasize both aspects. The second, "Applying Life Skills," is primarily a practical exercise.

This section builds on the understanding generated in the previous section. Students should be able to complete the exercise successfully by applying what they have just read.

Completing this section allows students to demonstrate their mastery of a specific life skill. It gives them the firsthand experience they need with tasks they are likely to encounter in everyday living.

An Answer Key at the back of the book helps students correct their work and gives them immediate feedback.

All units in each book are structured alike, each consisting of the six sections described here. Students quickly discover the regular pattern and are able to work with success and confidence throughout the text.

Use in Small-Group or Class Situations

Although the books in the Adult Learner Series were designed primarily for use on an individual basis, they can be used successfully in small-group or class situations. The comprehension, language and life skills questions can be adapted to whole-class instruction; this may be especially useful for students of English as a Second Language. If several students have read the stories, a group discussion may prove rewarding as well as motivating.

Writing Assignments

The comprehension questions and answers may also serve as suggestions for writing assignments.

For many students at this level, a writing assignment must be introduced in a very structured manner; otherwise, some students may find themselves unable to get started. On a group basis, the writing assignment may grow naturally out of the class discussion. In this case, the discussion may be all the introduction necessary.

On an individual basis, however, and also often within a group situation, it will be necessary to provide the student with a more concrete starting point. The teacher may find it necessary to provide model sentences or paragraphs, or to supply sentence beginnings ("If I had been there, I would have...") for the student to complete. The students can use their copies of the stories to search for word spellings, or the teacher may wish to write suggested words on the blackboard or provide a prepared list.

The Word List

Every word used in the story is included in the Word List, given alphabetically under the chapter in which it is first introduced. New forms that are made by adding the suffixes *-s*, *-ed*, *-ing*, and *-ly* to words that have already been introduced are indented.

The instructor may wish to scan the Word List to choose preview words in addition to the twenty in the Preview Words section at the beginning of each chapter. Non-phonetic words, which may present some difficulties in decoding, are printed in italics for quick indentification.

The Word List may also be used for the study of common sight words. Since an effort has been made to provide adequate repetition of each word, most of these words should be a solid part of the student's sight vocabulary by the time he or she has finished the story.

Summary of Chapters: The Secret of Room 401

Chapter 1: Into the Darkness *(Level 1.6)*

Rick Tardif's car goes off the road while he is hurrying home from work on a rainy night. The police arrive; he is taken by ambulance to the hospital. Rick is told that his back is broken and he may never walk again. Alice Marks, a spunky woman who is confined to a wheelchair, is introduced. Hospital workers Ed and Steve make plans and use a window shade signal.

Chapter 2: Out the Window *(Level 1.5)*

The next day, Rick finds out more about his condition and begins to get used to his "sandwich" bed. He becomes depressed and refuses to see his friends. He spots Ed giving the signal.

Chapter 3: On Watch (Level 1.6)

Rick sees Ed giving the signal again and becomes curious, but Ed doesn't return. At last Steve comes in and gives the signal. When the doctor announces that Rick will be moved to a new room, he refuses to go, since the signal mystery has become his only interest in life.

Chapter 4: Out of the Room (Level 1.8)

Alice and her granddaughter enjoy a faked escape attempt using sheets from the storeroom. Rick is moved into a revolving bed. He is taken to the physical therapy room but refuses to participate. Alice gets him to talk and then convinces him that life in a wheelchair can be worth living by sneaking out and buying him a pizza.

Chapter 5: Down the Hall (Level 1.5)

Alice teaches Rick how to push himself around on a rolling bed, using canes. Ed begs Steve not to hurt Rick. Rick gets Alice to watch for the two men; she reports that they are stealing drugs and insists on watching for them the next night.

Chapter 6: In Front of the Gun (Level 1.4)

Rick practices on the rolling bed. Ed and Steve change plans, then make their move. Ed catches Alice spying on them and calls Steve. Rick goes for help on the rolling bed, but Steve spots him. As Steve is about to shoot Alice, Rick startles him. Alice knocks Steve out, and the police come. Rick decides that he will go into physical therapy and try to walk again. He also welcomes a special visitor, his friend Kelly.

Words Introduced in the Story

Non-phonetic words are in italics. New forms of words already introduced are indented.

Chapter 1: Into the Darkness

a
about
accident
afraid
after
again
ahead
already
air
Alice
alive
all
almost
always
am
ambulance
an
and
another
any
anyone
anything
are
arm
around
as
asked
  asking
at
awake
away

baby
back
bad
  badly
bags
bank
basement
be
  being
bed
been
before
began
bent
big
bit
bleeding
bottom
breathing
bring
broken
burn
but
by

call
  called
came
can
can't
car
care

careful
  carefully
change
checked
climbed
  climbing
closed
coffee
come
  coming
could
couldn't
course
crash
cried
  crying
crushed
curve
cut
  cuts

Dad
dare
dark
darkness
days
date
dear
did
didn't
do

doing
doctor
  doctors
does
doesn't
don't
door
  doors
down
driver
driving
drop
drove

ear
eat
  eating
Ed
edge
elevator
else
emergency
end
enough
even
ever
every
everything

face
  faces
far
fast
father
feel
felt
few
fine

first
fix
flash
  flashed
fog
for
from
front

gas
gave
get
  gets
girl
give
glow
go
  going
gone
good
got
grab
  grabbed
Grandmother
guy

had
hall
hand
hanging
happen
  happened
hard
  harder
has
hate
have
he

head
  headed
headlights
heal
hear
held
hello
help
  helped
her
here
he's
hey
him
himself
his
hit
hole
home
hope
  hoped
  hoping
hospital
how
hurry
hurt

I
I'd
I'll
I'm
if
in
into
is
isn't
it
its

job
jumped
just

keep
  keeping
Kelly
kept
kind
kissed
knew
know
known

last
late
  later
lay
left
legs
let's
life
lifted
light
  lights
like
line
  lines
lit
little
live
long
look
  looked
  looking
  looks
lot
lying

mad
made
make
man
many
marks
may
me
mean
men
metal
might
mind
minute
  minutes
more
morning
mother
move
  moving
much
mud
  muddy
my

named
need
  needs
next
nice
night
no
not
nothing
now
nurse
  nurses

of

off
oh
  OK
on
one
only
open
  opened
or
other
out
outside
over

parking
part
people
phone
  picked
pictures
pill
pillow
pipe
play
police
policeman
  policemen
poor
pretty
pull
  pulled
pushed
put

quick
  quickly
quiet
  quietly

radio
rain
  raining
ran
reached
ready
real
  really
red
rest
Rick
Rick's
right
road
rocked
rolled
  rolling
roof
room
run
rushed
  rushing

sadly
said
same
say
  says
  saying
saw
second
see
seem
  seems
shade
she
shine
  shining

shone
shop
should
side
sight
silver
siren
sleep
slept
slid
slow
  slowly
smile
  smiled
  smiling
smoke
so
soft
  softly
some
someone
something
son
soon
  sooner
sorry
sped
spin
spun
standing
started
steep
stepped
Steve
still
stop
  stopped
strange

strapped
  straps
stretcher
suddenly
supper
sure
swung

take
  takes
talk
  talking
Tardif
tell
than
that
that's
the
their
them
then
there
these
they
they'll
they're
thing
  things
think
  thinking
this
those
thought
three
threw
through
till
time

times
tire
  tires
to
today
tomorrow
tonight
too
took
torch
touch
  touched
trees
truck
try
  tried
  trying
turned
two

under
up
use

wake
wait

waiting
walk
walking
wanted
was
wasn't
washed
watch
way
we
well
we'll
went
we're
were
weren't
wet
we've
what
what's
wheel
  wheels
wheelchair
when
where
while

who
why
wide
will
window
with
without
woman
won't
words
work
world
worry
would
wouldn't
wrecked
  wrecker

X-ray
  X-rays

yes
you
your
you're

Chapter 2: Out the Window

across
  arms
  ask

better
  babies
backbone
beat
behind

below
body
bottles
boy
boy's
brain
buckled
button

cars
cares
cast
chair
cheer
  close
cord
  cry

day
Dr.

eyes

fall
fear
fed
feed
  feeling
filled
find
flat
frame
friends

  getting
glad
good-by

hadn't
half
  hands
  happening
heard
helpless
herself
hold
hour
humming
hung

it's
itself

killed

let

lie
link
lower
lucky
lunch

  makes
maybe
  means
meant
middle
mirror
months
most
  moved
Mr.
Mrs.
must
myself

new

old
once

pad
parents
  partly
patted
place
person
  pulling
  push

questions

  Rains
relax
remember

remembered
rolling
rot

sat
scared
  seeing
shook
shout
  shouting
shut
  sitting
  sleepy
slipped
somehow
sometimes
sound
  sounded
spend
spinal
stood

  talked
teach
there's
they're
  thoughts
tied
tightly
tipped
  tired
top
tubes
  turn
TV

unbuckled
upset
  used

very

walked
waking
want
wash

watched
weak
which
white
wished
woke

wondered
worse

you'll

Chapter 3: On Watch

age
alone
along
asleep

bath
best
booth
  breathe
buzzer

cards
  check
cheerfully
cleans
clear
clock
cute

  dared
done
dragged

easy
  Ed's

fell
  filling
five

floor
forever
found
fun

giving
  guys

happy
  hardly
hide
  hours
  hurried

inside

least
letters
locks

matter
money
  month
mop

never
nights

often

pail
  pick

rats
read
risk
  rooms

  sees
  seemed
sent
shift
shoot
sick
signal
  sleeping
snapped
somewhere
stay
storeroom

taller
thank
thinner

  waited
  washing
ways
week

weeks
worked
working

wrong

yesterday

you'd
yourself

Chapter 4: Out of the Room

Alice's
Ann
Ann's
aren't
ate

bars
bought
box
boxes
brightly
burst

carrying
clean
closer
cold
crazy

dead
dove

everywhere

forget
forgot
full

ground

having
heading

healing
helping
hiding

I've

keeps

lady
lap
leaned
lift
living

making
meet
mine
Mom
mouth

neat
neatly

onto
ourselves

painful
pal
peeked
peeking
physical
picture

pile
piles
pizza
popping
pushing

ramps
rope

sad
safely
seen
sheet
sheets
shelves
short
slide
smelled
someday
stand
step
stop
stronger
stuck

therapy
tight
together
told
touching
trying
turning

unfolded
untie
upside-down

wall

waved
winked
wish
worth

you've

Chapter 5: Down the Hall

bet

canes
closet
creeps

dangerous
drugged
  drugs

fooling
footsteps
  funny

great

handles

haven't
himself
hooked
hug

key

locked
loud

missed
  mouths

ones
rang
running

scare
set
showed
  signals
  start
stealing
stole
surprised

  telling

wants
worried
wow

yet

Chapter 6: In Front of the Gun

against

because
believe
bounced
bullet

  calling
  cane
  crashed

creep
closing

danger
desk
downstairs

family

God

God's
gun

kill
killer

leaning
luck

married

mixed
moment
moves

near
  nearest
  nurses

past
  piled
  pointing

raised
  reach
rid
  roll

  safe
sake
saved
she's
shirt
shot
  show
slammed
  sliding
spot
straining
  strong

tests
  thanks
third
trigger
true

unlocked
unplugged

upstairs

  windows

yell

Answer Key

Comprehension Questions

Chapter 1
1. b	2. a	3. a	4. d	5. a
6. a	7. a	8. b	9. c	10. d

Chapter 2
1. b	2. a	3. b	4. d	5. b
6. a	7. c	8. c	9. b	10. b

Chapter 3
1. b	2. b	3. a	4. a	5. c
6. b	7. d	8. a	9. d	10. b

Chapter 4
1. a	2. c	3. a	4. c	5. d
6. d	7. a	8. a	9. b	10. b

Chapter 5
1. d	2. b	3. a	4. d	5. d
6. b	7. b	8. a	9. c	10. a

Chapter 6
1. c	2. c	3. c	4. a	5. b
6. d	7. a	8. a	9. c	10. d

Language Skills

Chapter 1: Exercise 1

1. _George Washington_

2. _John Adams_

3. _Thomas Jefferson_

4. _John Quincy Adams_

5. _Martin Van Buren_

6. _Abraham Lincoln_

7. _Woodrow Wilson_

8. _Warren G. Harding_

9. _Theodore Roosevelt_

Franklin D. Roosevelt

10. _F. D. R._

Exercise 2

1. James R. Grundy
2. Abe Klein
3. Dorothy Goodrich
4. Marie Curie
5. David Del Pozzo
6. Richard Almy
7. Diane Healy
8. Paul Gallagher
9. Bernadette De Rosa
10. Elizabeth T. Ethier

Chapter 2: Exercise 1

1. *Mr. Peter Blake*

2. *Mrs. Gloria Downes*

3. *Miss Mary Kelly*

4. *Ms. Sonia Rojski*

Exercise 2
   1. President
   2. president
   3. Vice President
   4. vice president

Exercise 3
   1. representative
   2. Representative
   3. Treasurer
   4. treasurer
   5. Postmaster
   6. postmaster

Chapter 3: Exercise 1

1. Thomas Way

2. Rivera Avenue .

3. Morton Road

4. Longwood Avenue

5. Window Drive

Exercise 2

1. Phoenix, Arizona

2. Dover, Delaware

3. Madison, Wisconsin

4. Baltimore, Maryland

5. Boston, Massachusetts

Exercise 3

1. _Denver CO_
2. _Miami FL_
3. _Dayton OH_
4. _New York NY_
5. _Chicago IL_

Chapter 4: Exercise 1

1. _Pacific Ocean_
2. _Mississippi River_
3. _Columbia River_
4. _Arctic Ocean_
5. _Lake Erie_
6. _Lake Huron_

Exercise 2

1. _Andes Mountains._
2. _Laurentian Mountains._
3. _Mount Everest_
4. _Vancouver Island_
5. _Aleutian Islands_
6. _Long Island_

Exercise 3

1. _France_
2. _China_
3. _South Africa_
4. _Venezuela_
5. _Australia_
6. _Canada_

Chapter 5: Exercise 1

1. *Sunday*

2. *Saturday*

3. *Thursday*

4. *Wednesday*

5. *Tuesday*

Exercise 2

1. *June*

2. *May*

3. *February*

4. *September*

5. *November*

Exercise 3
1. winter
2. autumn
3. fall
4. summer
5. spring

Chapter 6: Exercise 1

1. _English_
2. _French_
3. _Latin_
4. _Chinese_
5. _German_
6. _Russian_

Exercise 2
  1. geography 2

  Geography 2

  2. biology 3

  Biology 3

  3. cooking 1

  Cooking 1

  4. typing 5

  Typing 5

  5. history 1

  History 1

  6. geometry 2

  Geometry 2

Exercise 3
  1. shorthand
  2. biology
  3. typing

  4. woodworking
  5. civics
  6. history

Chapter 1

1. C-4

2. C-9

3. C-2

4. C-8

5. Smart Shopping

6. Diet Menus

7. Thinking About Your Health

8. Knowing Your Wines

Chapter 2

1. _Sozio's Supermarket_

5. _4_

6. _16_

7. a. _$1_

  b. _25¢_

8. a. _Cream Style_

  b. _Whole Kernel_

Chapter 3

1. _Shopwell Market_
2. _Skimmed Milk_
3. _2_

   a half-gallon
4. _$2_
5. _$7.50_
6. _Good February 26 - March 4, 1995_
7. _1_
8. _With this coupon_

Chapter 4

1. *USE IN ANY STORE* .

2. *General Products Corporation*

3. *August 31, 1995*

4. *40¢*

Chapter 5

1. *4 pounds*

2. *$2.00*

3. *pound*

4. *3 pounds*

5. *$3.00* .

6. *$1.00*

pound

Applying Life Skills

Chapter 1

1. _C-7_

2. _C-3_

3. _C-9_

4. _C-8_

5. _C-2_

6. _C-6_

7. _C-4_

8. _C-5_

Chapter 2

1. <u>**4**</u>

   <u>**15½**</u>

   <u>**$1**</u>

   <u>*Regular*</u>

   <u>French Style</u>

2. <u>**3**</u>

   <u>**17**</u>

   <u>**$1**</u>

   <u>Medium Small</u>

3. <u>**3**</u>

   <u>**15**</u>

   <u>**$1**</u>

   <u>*Cut*</u>

4. <u>**4**</u>

   <u>**16**</u>

   <u>**$1**</u>

   <u>Sliced</u>

5. <u>*Corn*</u>

   <u>Green Beans</u>

   <u>Beets</u>

   <u>**25¢**</u>

6. <u>Sweet Peas</u>

   <u>Wax Beans</u>

   <u>**33⅓¢**</u>

Chapter 3

1. _Shop and Save_
2. _Yogurt_
3. _3_

   8 ounces
4. _34¢_
5. _#5_
6. _February 26 - March 4, 1995_
7. _1_
8. _With this coupon_

Chapter 4

1. _Use in any store_
2. _QUICK SOUP_
3. _This coupon is good for any size or flavor_

4. _a. no_

   b. yes

5. _Limit : 1 to a customer_

6. _December 31, 1995_

Chapter 5: Chart 1

1. _20¢_

2. _30¢_

3. _40¢_

Chart 2

1. _$1.00_

2. _$1.50_

3. _$2.50_

Comparing Charts

1. *pound*
2. *40¢*
3. *10¢*

   pound

Chapter 6

1. *7 ounces*
2. *1*
3. *240*
4. *50 grams*
5. *110%*
6. *0 grams*
7. *3 grams*
8. *0%*
9. *40%*
10. *50%*
11. *4%*

Comprehension Progress Graph

How to Use the Comprehension Progress Graph

1. At the top of the graph, find the number of the chapter you have just read.
2. Follow the line down until it crosses the line for the number of questions you got right.
3. Put a dot • where the lines cross.
4. The numbers on the other side of the graph show your comprehension score.

For example, this graph shows the score of a student who answered 7 questions right for Chapter 1. The score is 70%. →

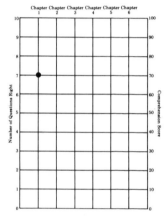

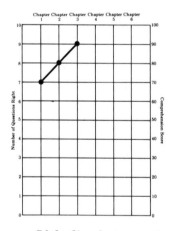

This same student got scores of 80% and 90% on Chapters 2 and 3. The line connecting the dots keeps going up. This shows that the student is doing well. ←

If the line between the dots on your graph does not go up, or if it goes down, see your instructor for help.

Comprehension Progress

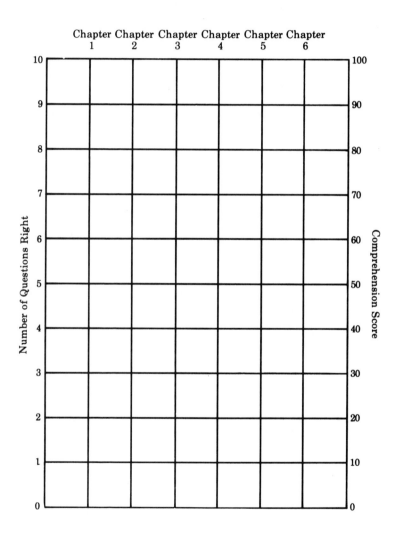

Skills Profile Graph

How to Use the Skills Profile Graph

1. There is a block on this graph for every comprehension question in the book.

2. Every time you get a question wrong, fill in a block which has the same letter as the question you got wrong. For example, if you get an A question wrong, fill in a block in the A row. Use the right row for each letter.

Look at the graph. It shows the profile of a student who got 3 questions wrong. This student got an A question wrong, a C question wrong, and a D question wrong.

On the next chapter, this same student got 4 questions wrong and has filled in 4 more blocks.

The graph now looks like this. This student seems to be having trouble on question C. This shows a reading skill that needs to be worked on.

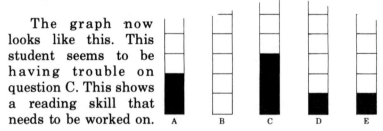

The blocks that are filled in on your graph tell you and your instructor the kinds of questions that give you trouble.

Look for the rows that have the most blocks filled in. These rows will be higher than the others. Talk to your instructor about them. Your instructor may want to give you extra help on these skills.

Skills Profile

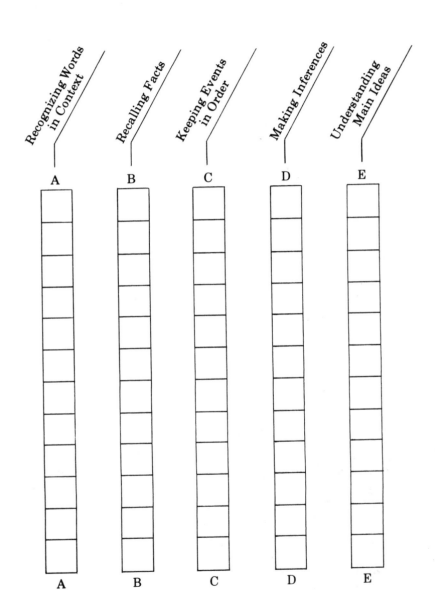